The IT Business Owner's Survival Guide

The IT Business Owner's Survival Guide

How to save time, avoid stress and build a successful IT business

Richard Tubb

Disclaimer: The author assumes no responsibility for the use or misuse of this product, or for any injury, damage and/or financial loss sustained to persons or property as a direct or indirect result of using this report. The author cannot guarantee your future results and/or success, as there are some unknown risks in business and on the Internet that we cannot foresee. The use of the information contained in this book should be based on your own due diligence, and you agree that the author is not liable for any success or failure of your business that is directly or indirectly related to the purchase and use of this information.

First printing: 2016

ISBN-13: 978-1523856275
ISBN-10: 1523856270

British Cataloguing Publication Data:
A catalogue record of this book is available from The British Library.

Contents

Chapter 1: What to do when you have too much to do, but don't know where to start

"I've got too much to do" and "I wish I had more time" are two of the most common complaints I hear from exasperated and stressed out IT business owners. It's true that as the head honcho in your IT business, you almost certainly do have an awful lot that needs doing. But solving that challenge by wishing for more time? Trust me when I say that however hard you wish, you'll never find more than 24 hours in the day.

With that said, in this chapter I'm going to help you learn how to pull yourself out from under. When you reach a stage where you have so much to do that you don't know where to start, at best you focus on doing whatever is most urgent (typically client work) rather than what is important (business and personal growth), and at worst you can become frozen with indecision and not do anything at all.

Getting out from under

If you're feeling overwhelmed with too many things to do and not sure where to start, then the most important thing you can do right now is to empty your head and get everything down on paper.

Brew yourself a warm drink (for me it's always green tea), find yourself a quiet spot (the office, before anyone gets in often works) and sit yourself down with a plain A4 writing pad and a pen.

Naturally, using a pen and paper will feel a strangely odd choice for someone who works in IT, so to scratch that itch you almost certainly have to use technology somehow. Turn your smartphone to aeroplane mode (we don't want to be disturbed) and fire up the stopwatch app. Set it to 25 minutes and set it counting down.

For the next 25 minutes you are going to write down everything you can possibly think of that you need to get done. That's everything that needs to be done within your business, from putting out the rubbish to cleaning out your inbox, from filing the company taxes to setting a marketing plan.

If you're struggling with where to begin, think of your top three clients. Write down any outstanding requests they may have made, be they requests for technical support, requests for quotes, or requests for advice.

Pretty soon you'll be on a roll. At this stage don't worry about the size of the tasks you are writing down, or how you will achieve them. Just write.

Don't restrict yourself to work related tasks either. If you need to go shopping for groceries later in the week, write down everything you think you will need. If you keep meaning to decorate the living room, jot that job down. If your pet cat needs a new flea collar, put that down too.

The exercise here is to do a brain dump and get everything out of your head and onto paper. Don't worry about the order you've written the tasks down in. Just empty your brain.

All done? How much better does that feel now?

The human brain is a powerful thing and you can remember a lot of things, but it's not very good at being a task list. The more things you keep in your head, the less likely you are to remember what is important. Or, even if you remember what is important, you'll have a nagging feeling that you're forgetting something else.

As we progress through our Survival Guide, remember that the more things you write down or store on a list, the more your brain is freed up to do important work. Talking of lists, we'll look at how to organise that big disorganised list of tasks in our next section, but for now, pat yourself on the back and go about your normal business. No, really. Go and watch TV. Go and fix a PC. Turn your smartphone out of aeroplane mode and marvel as the world coped without you for 25 minutes.

I virtually guarantee that by the time you return to our next section you'll probably have thought of another half dozen things to add to your list (but don't try to think of them now, your brain doesn't work that way).

How to build a To-Do List that actually gets things done

As we've already mentioned, the brain is not a good place to store the multitude of things you want to get done. Trying to do something while trying to remember to do something else afterwards doesn't work well. As human beings, we're pretty bad at multitasking. We work far better when we focus on one thing at a time.

Most of us are familiar with To-Do lists, even if it's something as basic as a list of groceries we want to buy at the store. Having a list means we don't have to worry about remembering what we need to do; we just need to look at the list and be reminded.

The trouble is, for most of us, life's To-Do list isn't as simple as a few tasks that need knocking off sequentially. Our To-Do list grows every day and quite often we build a list that is so big, with so many items on it, that we struggle to know where to start and are often frozen by indecision.

In this chapter I want to help you build a To-Do list that – well, gets stuff done! We'll work from the Brainstorm list we built earlier on – that page (or pages!) of items that we got out of our head in no discernible order.

Let's grab another sheet of A4 paper and a pen. Now, before we begin, I hear the technician in you asking if this wouldn't be a good time to use an app instead of pen and paper. Don't worry, we'll get to the To-Do apps in our next section – but before we do that, we need to know how we're going to set up the app we decide upon. This is where we decide how our To-Do lists look.

On our fresh sheet of A4 paper I want you to write down a series of contexts for the type of To-Dos you typically create, proceeded by the squiggly 'at' sign. For instance, I typically create To-Dos that remind me to...

- Do things at home (@Home)
- Do things at the office (@Office)
- Do things for clients (@Client Work)
- Call certain people (@Calls)
- Remind me that I'm waiting on someone for something (@Waiting For)
- Do certain errands (@Errands)

Your list of contexts probably looks something similar. Feel free to add your own, but try not to add too many – we don't want to freeze our brains trying to work out which context a To-Do should be added to!

With our list of contexts in hand, let's grab our earlier Brainstorm list and methodically work through it, deciding which context the item belongs in. If we've written "Call Dave" then that belongs on the @Calls list. If we need to shred that paperwork from our in-tray, then that belongs on the @Office list. If we need to pick up some shopping items, that belongs on the @Errands list. And so on.

The value of using contexts

Why are we grouping our tasks together in this way? Quite simply, when it comes to actually doing things (as opposed to creating lists of things we want to do!) then you'll quickly find that batching items together gets stuff done a lot quicker. For instance, for those of us who find it difficult to pick up the telephone, it's easier to knock off 3 or 4 telephone calls in quick succession than it is to make a number of single calls throughout the day.

In a similar vein, having contexts to our To-Do list allows us to reduce the decision making that goes into choosing what we need to do next, and adjust for our swings in mood and energy. If we're in the office and feeling a bit low, we can choose to waste our time looking at videos of cats on Facebook, or we can hit up our @Office list and work on some low energy tasks that we need to complete. That shredding. Or sorting your in-tray. What you'll probably find is that by getting something productive done (and not giggling at cats on Facebook) and subsequently knocking an item off your To-Do list in this way, you'll probably be inspired to tackle something else.

So now we have our Brainstorm list of items. We have our list of contexts that are personalised for our typical tasks, and we've categorised our brainstorm list of items into those contexts. Next, let's choose a high tech and productive method to keep our To-Do lists organised and managed, wherever we are...

Further reading

- Getting Things Done (revised edition) by David Allen – http://tubb.co/GTDRevised

- Mind Mapping by Tony Buzan – http://www.tonybuzan.com/about/mind-mapping/
- 21 Ways To Manage The Stuff That Sucks Up Your Time by Grace Marshall – http://tubb.co/21WaysGMBook

What productivity tool should I use?

Finally! We've come to the bit that most technicians feel most comfortable with and enjoy doing when it comes to being productive. Spending time choosing an app to manage their To-Do lists!

Many of us who have tried to get organised before and failed know the dangers of focusing too much on the tool we will use to be productive, and not enough time on, you know, actually being productive!

To be blunt, the tool you use to keep your notes, reminders and To-Dos doesn't matter as much as the methodology you use. We've already discussed our methodology – brainstorming to empty our head and using context to determine where tasks belong and what to do at any given time – so whether you end up putting this information into a PC, a smartphone, or even just a good old fashioned notebook (more on using pen and paper later in this section), you'll find you get more things done.

With that said, most of us nowadays live life at full pace and on the move. It therefore makes sense for us to use apps that enable us to read and update our To-Do lists and reminders from wherever we are.

When choosing a productivity tool it's important to remember that our productive lives typically revolve around 3 areas – our calendar, our inbox and our To-Do lists. Any tool we choose should have some level of integration between the three, to make our lives easier.

If you're a Microsoft Outlook user, then you've already got your tool. Microsoft Outlook has a powerful calendar function, strong features to help you manage your overflowing inbox (more on managing your email in a later chapter) and a To-Do list (or "Task list" in Microsoft speak) that can be customised to feature the various @ contexts we looked at earlier.

If you're a Google Apps user, or simply not a fan of Microsoft Outlook, then you'll probably want to check out some different but complementary tools that can help you become organised. Google Apps is great for email (again, more on managing email later in the book) and has a flexible calendar tool. Google Apps To-Do list functionality is not so strong – and so a separate third party app might be preferable. For myself, I use Google Mail, Google Calendar and a tool called Remember The Milk (RTM). RTM is a simple-to-use app that enables me to create various lists to match my personal context preferences, which can then be accessed via an app on my Android smartphone or tablet (iOS and Windows Apps are also available) or via a web browser from any PC or other device. RTM synchronises your To-Do list between devices, so wherever and however you access your To-Do list – it's up to date.

Aside from RTM, other popular To-Do list tools include Todoist, Wunderlist, Asana and AllThings, each of which have their own strengths. For instance, AllThings is very strong at allowing your lists to be shared between colleagues and so is popular amongst IT and marketing companies.

Take a look at a few tools – most apps are free for the basic product, so try as many as you like – and go with your gut feeling over the one that has the look and feel that suits you most.

Further Reading

Remember The Milk (RTM) – https://www.rememberthemilk.com

- Google Apps for Work – https://www.google.com/work/apps/business/
- AllThings – http://www.allthings.io/tubblog
- Todoist – https://en.todoist.com/
- Wunderlist – https://www.wunderlist.com/
- Asana – https://asana.com/

How to share tasks with colleagues

We've briefly mentioned sharing To-Do lists and tasks with colleagues. While I'd always recommend using a single trusted system for all of your info (reducing the options over making a decision on where something belongs is a powerful way to get stuff done) you may end up using two or three different productivity tools for different purposes – especially for those tasks which you want your colleagues to be aware of. For instance, if your IT business is using a Professional Services Automation (PSA) tool such as Autotask and ConnectWise, or a basic helpdesk system, you'll be familiar with ticket boards or queues. These boards or queues are where you record things that you need to do within your business, or tasks you want to track the time spent on.

These boards are typically used for client facing or technical work. It's not unusual for an IT business to have a "Helpdesk" board with client support requests, a "Monitoring" board for automated troubleshooting alerts from client sites, and a "Sales" board for opportunities. You might consider adding to your queues with an "Internal" board.

An "Internal" board is used for those things that your business needs to do for itself. These tasks might be administrative, technical or any other nature. Think of the "Internal" board as the queue for treating your business as its own client. For instance, if you've upgraded all the PCs in your office and the old PCs need decommissioning for disposal then raise a ticket on the "Internal" board to do this. By doing so, you've got the task out of your head and into a place where your colleagues can be aware of it. After all, the job of decommissioning old PCs probably isn't the best use of your time as an IT business owner (you might disagree, but we'll look at the art of delegation later). If this type of task is on your personal To-Do list, you'll feel responsible for its completion. If it's on your IT business' "Internal" board then responsibility for it can be assigned to anyone within your team and you can keep track of the progress of the job through the normal ticket updates.

Further Reading

- Autotask – http://www.autotask.com/
- ConnectWise – http://www.connectwise.com/

Building a brilliant To-Do list

So we have still got our Brainstorm list of items that need doing. We've decided upon a set of contexts (@Home, @Office, etc.) that we feel will work for us. We've taken a look at the various productivity tools on the market and made a decision on the one we will use (even if it's just for now). And we've considered the potential of an "Internal" board in our PSA or helpdesk system, and decided whether or not to implement it for our own IT business. In short, we've created a system that will help us stay organised going forwards. Congratulations!

Our next step is to populate our new system with what's already on our plate, and begin using it on a day-to-day basis.

If you haven't already, go ahead and populate your To-Do list with the various contexts you decided upon. If you're using Microsoft Outlook, that will mean creating some task categories such as

@Home and @Office. If you're using RTM or another third party app, create the various sub-lists titled @Home, @Calls, etc.

Now we're going to revisit our Brainstorm list and methodically move the tasks into the appropriate area on our To-Do list. While our Brainstorm list probably included some brief outlines – such as "Memory Upgrade" – it's important when we transcribe our Brainstorm list items onto our To-Do list that we use descriptive "doing" statements.

By using "doing" statements, you're setting yourself up to achieve more on a day-to-day basis. So while you might recall what "Memory Upgrade" means now, when you come to actually get that task done, will you remember what type of memory you need and where to buy it from?

For instance, if you've written down "Memory Upgrade" on your Brainstorm list then when you transcribe this task onto your To-Do list you may write "Buy Memory Upgrades for PC". If you're not sure what memory upgrade you need then you may write "Research Memory Upgrade needed for PC" instead. If you do know what type of memory upgrade you need, you may write "Buy 16GB SoDIMM Memory Upgrade for PC from Computer 2000" – specifying exactly what you are buying and from which supplier.

In a nutshell, any tasks you transcribe from your Brainstorm to your To-Do list should be a "doing" statement explaining the next step you'll take – reducing your resistance to actually doing it when the time comes.

Go ahead and transcribe your Brainstorm list to your To-Do list now using "doing" statements. Don't get distracted by actually trying to do any of those things you're transcribing, even if they are quickies. For now just concentrate on populating your To-Do list with everything you want to get done.

Why you should use an Attention Log

Congratulations on emptying your head with your Brainstorm list, and building your first real, actual, will-actually-work To-Do list full of "doing" tasks!

At this stage, you're probably feeling much calmer about everything you need to do and have greater clarity of how you're going to get those things done. You'll be full of enthusiasm to get going!

Before you get going, I want to encourage you to consider using an Attention Log.

While brainstorming is a useful process that helps empty our heads of dozens of things, and in fact is something we should do fairly regularly, on a day-to-day basis there will be things buzzing around our heads – ideas, people to call, things to do – that we know we need to remember.

Some of the time those things will pop into our heads when we're in front of the PC or have our smartphone to hand and can immediately add them to our To-Do list.

But other times those pesky thoughts pop into our heads when we're unable to add them to our To-Do list. While we're driving, while we're out walking, while we're lying in bed, while we're at a family meal or in a meeting.

When these thoughts crop up and you're unable to note them in your To-Do list – either because it's impractical or you'd be breaking etiquette – don't make the mistake of thinking "That's ok, I'll remember that". At best you'll remember some of those things. Or you'll remember there is something you need to remember, but can't remember what it was.

Instead, start using an Attention Log.

An Attention Log (or Logs, if you decide that works for you) is somewhere for you to dump those thoughts so you don't have to remember them, and then at a later date add them to your To-Do list properly.

For instance, in every room of my house I have pen and paper, which allows me to jot down thoughts. I have pen and paper next to my bed, so when I'm lying staring at the ceiling, unable to get to sleep with something on my mind, I write it down, empty my head (secure in the knowledge the written thought will be waiting for me in the morning) and drift off to sleep.

I also take a small notepad and pencil to business meetings. While tapping at a keyboard or smartphone may be considered bad etiquette at a meeting, writing brief notes on a pad is not considered as such.

As well as old fashioned pen and paper Attention Logs, I also use the electronic equivalent – Evernote. (If you're a Microsoft fan, you might take a look at OneNote, which is very similar.)

Evernote allows you to capture all manner of things from different sources. You can clip websites to a note. You can write freeform notes. You can record voice to a note. Evernote is a great way to dump content that you want to refer back to later. For instance, when I'm driving and inspiration strikes me, I can record a voice snippet into Evernote with details of my thoughts.

Once a week (at least) schedule some time to do a sweep of all your Attention Logs. Gather all those bits of paper from around the house, whip out your notebook, fire up Evernote. Then transcribe those notes into your To-Do list. Then start again for a new week with fresh Attention Logs.

So whether it's pen or paper, Evernote or something else – find ways of capturing those thoughts that ping into your head at any time of day or night. Getting them out of your head is hugely important. Remember, the human brain doesn't do well at being a To-Do list.

How to stop putting things off

Congratulations! We now have an honest-to-goodness, real-life, actual, proper To-Do list that is tailored to our specific needs using contexts that are relevant to us.

At this stage we're ready to roll up our sleeves and get on with getting some of those tasks done so we can bask in the warm glow of being a productivity expert!

Except... we might be looking at the list and thinking "Holy cow! It's just too much! I'll just check out Facebook for a minute or two." A minute or two turns into 30 minutes, which turns into a morning, and by the end of the day we're panicking, feeling guilty and cursing the fact we've spent another day doing everything but what actually needed to be done!

I speak from experience here. To this day I struggle with procrastination. In fact, when it came to writing this chapter, I had to fight against the resistance to do something else (anything else) instead of sitting down to write.

But I did get this chapter written, and you can find ways to stop putting things off and doing what needs to be done too! Here are some techniques you can use yourself.

Batching Tasks

Quite often we have a number of tasks that are similar in nature – typically things like making telephone calls to a variety of people, or dealing with an overflowing inbox full of emails.

Wherever possible, look for opportunities to batch these tasks together. Batching such tasks makes it easier to shift your focus to a specific type of task and get multiple tasks knocked off quickly and efficiently.

Take telephone calls, for instance. Making that call to a client to discuss renewing their contract may be something you've been putting off. You may also need to call your vendor account manager to ask him a question. Oh, and you keep meaning to phone your Mum but never seem to find the time!

By pulling these three tasks together in a batch and deciding to do them one after the other, you'll find a rhythm that will reduce the resistance you may have experienced trying to make each of those calls individually. On your To-Do list, each of those tasks should be listed on your @Calls context list in a "doing" manner, such as:

- Call Alan @ Draymech – Tel: 0121 603 818 – Re: Firmware Upgrades
- Call Mum at home – Catch-up
- Call Dave Steel @ Steelline – Tel: 07988 3551 – Re: Contract renewal

By writing down those tasks in a "doing" manner, when it came to actually doing those tasks and calling those people, you eliminated the need to scratch your head and remind yourself why you needed to call the person, or the need to scurry off to your address book to find the right telephone numbers (I'm going to presume you know your Mum's telephone number off by heart).

In our batched list of calls, why not telephone your Mum first to say hello? Such a call is easy to make, and some way into the call you may even find yourself wanting to bring the call to a close so you can call your client!

Once you've put down the phone on that first call, immediately dial the next person on the list. This way, you'll find the call easier to initiate and you may find that you're already "in the flow" and find it easier to chat too.

I've used telephone calls as an example of using the batching technique, but it works for just about anything you may need to do. Keep an eye out for opportunities to batch jobs together, and revel in the feeling of knocking multiple tasks off in a single go!

Breaking bigger tasks down into smaller steps

Have you ever looked at a task and thought "I don't know where to start?"

I know I have. Even tasks that are written in a "doing" way can feel insurmountable. For instance, "Replace Server at Steeltech" is a "doing" statement, but replacing a server surely isn't something to be done in a single step!

Whenever you come across a task and you are filled with the desire to skip over it and say "Maybe later!" then consider if that task needs breaking down into smaller steps.

For instance, "Replace Server at Steeltech" is a big project. But what's the one thing you need to do to get it started? I'm not talking about starting AND finishing the job – but the very next thing you'd need to do to set yourself on the path to getting the job done.

In this example, it may be "Order New Server for Steeltech from Draymech". Or, in reality, even that task may feel a bit too big.

Maybe our next step is actually "Specify New Server for Steeltech".

Now, sitting down to spec up a new server for a client feels a lot more achievable than "Replace Server", doesn't it?

Once you've finished specifying the new server, your next step may now be "Order New Server for Steeltech". Or, in reality, you may be thinking "But I don't know which supplier to order the server from!" So rewrite the task as "Get Quotes from Draymech, Computer 99 and Eastcoast for Server for Steeltech".

Whenever you're writing a task down, as well as using "doing" language, also make the job as small as possible to reduce your resistance to getting started and your stress levels at knowing how and where to start.

This takes practice. To begin with you'll continue to write down things like "New Server for Steeltech". Then you'll get into the habit of writing in "doing" language – "Replace Server at Steeltech". Finally, you'll get into the habit of breaking the task down into the smallest of steps – "Specify New Server for Steeltech".

By acquiring the habit of breaking tasks down into the smallest possible steps, you'll quickly find you overcome the resistance to getting started on any task at all, and thumb your nose at procrastination!

Using the Pomodoro technique

In my experience, even when you're using "doing" language to list your To-Do list, and even when you've broken big tasks down into smaller chunks, resistance to being productive can still lurk around every corner. "I just don't feel like doing it!" whispers the whiny voice in your head. Browsing Facebook once again feels like a good idea, and once again procrastination looks to have won the day!

But wait. Help is at hand and it's in the shape of a tomato!

The Pomodoro Technique is a time management method that breaks work down into intervals of 25 minutes – intervals known as Pomodori, which is the plural of the Italian word for tomato.

The idea behind the Pomodoro Technique is that by working for just 25 minutes, followed by a break, you're much more likely to get started (25 minutes is nothing, right?) and also discourages you from practising perfectionism – the scourge of the Productivity Ninja! By setting yourself an artificial deadline of 25 minutes, you will find that you are more focused on getting something done inside those 25 minutes.

In reality, I find the Pomodoro Technique a great way to just get started on any task, and if I get to the end of the 25 minutes and I'm "in the flow", I continue anyway!

So do yourself a favour and invest in an electronic kitchen timer (you could use your smartphone, but trust me, you'll get distracted by all the other things it's capable of doing). Set it to 25 minutes and get started on that task you've been putting off.

Thank you, Italian tomato! The most productive of all the healthy food world!

Further Reading

- How to End Procrastination with the Pomodoro Technique – http://tubb.co/1OjB7Hn
- Mini LCD Digital Cooking Timer – http://tubb.co/1DknEIQ
- How to Stop Putting Things Off – http://tubb.co/1J9oUFf

Writing down 3 things to get done today

Even with well written and maintained To-Do lists, it can be difficult to pick the right thing to be doing on any given day. There is a danger that you cherry pick and select the tasks you want to do, as opposed to the tasks that you need to do.

One way to make sure you stay on focus with the most urgent or important tasks is, every day, to write down the 3 things you must get done today. Typically, these are tasks that are either important (definitely needs doing soon) or urgent (must get done today!).

Make sure you only write 3 tasks, not 4, not 6 and not 10. While the desire to be super-productive may be strong, reality is a killer. It's my experience that if you complete 3 written tasks, and then go on to do another 3, you'll feel like a winner. But if you write down 10 tasks and only complete 6, at the end of the day you'll feel bad about the tasks you didn't complete.

I'd recommend you write down your tasks on a simple sheet of paper. If you wanted to be super smart and send a message to all passers-by that you are indeed a productivity expert, you can buy a notepad that has "Things to do today!" already written boldly on it! On my desk I use a yellow coloured pad by Niceday (No. 184866) which allows me to write down the 3 things that, if I completed today, I'd feel like the day was well spent.

Then you work on completing those 3 tasks ahead of anything else that falls in your lap. Sure, you may be interrupted by telephone calls, distracted by colleagues, or bothered by meetings – but when you return from that distraction, you know what you need to work on to make the day a success.

Remember to use "doing" language when writing your three tasks for the day, and break tasks down into the smallest step you can think of.

Scheduling tasks in your calendar

All this talk of To-Do lists, and we're neglecting one of the most powerful weapons for ensuring we get things done – our calendar.

It goes without saying that you'd be crazy to try to remember appointments, places you need to be, and people you need to see, all in your head. Remember, the human brain isn't good at To-Do lists. Most of us, therefore, set appointments in our calendar specifying who we're meeting, where we are meeting them, and why we're meeting them. Whenever I set an appointment in Google Calendar, I also like to invite external parties to the meeting – making sure the time goes into their diary as well as mine.

But you can also use your calendar to remind you of things that need to be done on a certain day. Now, I'm not talking about things that need to be done BY a certain date – such as your tax return being sent off before a deadline. I'm talking about those tasks that can't be done before, often can't be done after, and must be done on a certain day. "Telephone my sister Ruth to wish her a happy birthday" is a task that must be done on a certain date. It's doubtful Ruth would appreciate a call to wish her a happy birthday as much the day before, and she certainly wouldn't appreciate being called the day after her birthday. No, calling Ruth on her birthday is the only thing to do.

But as well as using our calendar to remind us of things that must be done on a certain day, we can also use it to block out time to get our own stuff done.

Given the opportunity, your days will fill up with everything that other people want you to do. Meeting invitations, telephone calls, emails, support tickets. If you're not careful, you'll never get anything important done, and constantly respond to what is perceived to be urgent.

So if you do have something important that needs doing, don't wait until it's urgent. Schedule it in your calendar now and treat it like you would a meeting with someone else: immovable.

If you need 25 minutes to put together that important quote for a new client – block out 25 minutes in your diary to do it. When you get asked if you can meet with someone at that same time, politely inform them: "I'm sorry, I've got a prior engagement at that time."

When the time comes, treat that time as you would a meeting. Turn off your phone, tell people you're busy, and concentrate on the job at hand. If you were meeting someone in your office, you wouldn't take telephone calls or chat with coworkers, would you? Treat this "meeting" in the same way.

Scheduling time in your diary is an important tactic that you can use to make sure the important gets done before it becomes urgent.

Chapter 2:
How to cope with too much email

When did my job become doing email?

If you're old enough to remember when email was shiny and new (which I'm sure you're unlikely to be, as it's a well-known fact most IT business owners are both young and terribly good looking) then you'll recall that back in the day email was typically used by just a few to share important information across great distances, spanning different time zones.

Today, your colleague sitting at the desk next to you is just as likely to email you asking which sandwich you'd like for lunch rather than bother getting out of their seat and talking to you.

Electronic communication, and email in particular, is seen by many as the scourge of the modern age. We're forever being interrupted by notifications of new messages, bombarded with information (most of which we don't need, nor want) and email is often wrongly used when that much more old fashioned method of communication – talking to one another – would be more effective.

If your inbox is overflowing and you're asking the question "When did my job become doing email?", then I've got good news for you – relief is at hand.

The bad news is you're going to need to break some pretty bad habits to bring email under control. For the majority of us, email makes us feel important – and so we secretly like the fact that we get a lot of email. Who doesn't like to feel in demand by others?

The trouble with this mindset is, it turns our inbox into a To-Do list that is dictated to us by others.

So how can we change this and regain control over our email?

Don't Graze Email

The first bad habit we need to break is the continuous grazing of email that we are seemingly addicted to.

Dipping in and out of your inbox all day, every day, is a recipe for being unproductive, all day, every day.

Admittedly, there are some jobs that require you to monitor email continuously. Manning the helpdesk is one. Being an IT business owner is not.

Firstly, build the habit of checking in on your email at set intervals. If you're a fan of the Pomodoro Technique that we discussed in an earlier chapter – working on set tasks for 25 minutes before taking a break – then you might check email in between those Pomodoris. My personal preference would be to check email 2 or 3 times a day – say, 11am, again at 2pm and one final time at 4pm.

Speaking as a former IT business owner myself, I can say with a great degree of confidence that NO email cannot afford to wait 25 minutes. In fact, in my experience, most emails don't need to be responded to inside 2 hours. I'd say that if something is truly urgent, the person trying to contact you via email will pick up the telephone instead.

For most of us, we check email on our smartphone as soon as we roll out of bed. Again, experience tells me this is a terrible habit. Instead of waking up with an idea of what you want to achieve for the day, you're immediately looking to email and external sources to dictate to you what they need you to be doing. Even if you read an email first thing in the morning and try to ignore it, you'll find it's subconsciously gnawing away at your attention – and you'll be distracted until you give that email the attention it desires. No, don't check your email until you've got at least one good task completed – the first of your three things to do today (see Chapter One).

Further Reading

- How to end procrastination with the Pomodoro Technique – http://tubb.co/1OjB7Hn

Turn off Email Notifications

The second bad habit we need to break is the Pavlovian Dog way we respond to email notifications.

Have you ever been in a meeting with a friend, or worse, a client, and heard your smartphone ping to tell you that you have a new message? Do you have a strong urge to just briefly check what that message is, and who the message is from? Do you give in to those urges, checking your phone even though your friend or client is talking to you? We've all been there – but you can make sure you're not "that" person by turning off notifications.

If you're a Microsoft Outlook user, then turn desktop alerts off so you aren't distracted by continuous pop-ups of tantalizing new emails in your Windows taskbar. While you're at it, turn off the notification sound too.

If you're a Google Mail or other webmail service user, turn off the numbered notification that appears in your web browser. You don't need to be distracted knowing how many emails are waiting for you.

Don't forget your smartphone. Whether you're an iPhone, Android or Windows Phone user, turn off the notification sound, the icon notification, and don't forget the LED notification too. If you're a Blackberry user, you're probably so addicted to email that you're beyond help. Seek professional counselling. (I'm kidding, of course, Blackberry users – turn off those notifications too.)

Becoming disconnected from email notifications will feel awkward at first. What if there is an important email waiting for me? What if somebody is trying to contact me urgently? I'll just take a quick peek to make sure that everything is ok...

Try disconnecting yourself from email notifications as an experiment. Give it a go for a week. If you experience no email disasters, why not try staying disconnected from email notifications for another week? Pretty soon you'll realise that your addiction to email is one of the biggest things holding you back from genuinely being productive as an IT business owner, and you can do without it.

Further Reading

- AwayFind – https://www.awayfind.com/ – Let urgent emails cut through the clutter and find you.
- Turning off Outlook notifications – http://www.howtogeek.com/80052/quick-tip-turn-off-desktop-email-notifications-in-outlook-2/
- Turning off Gmail notifications – http://www.wikihow.com/Disable-Gmail-Desktop-Notifications

How to process email effectively

How many emails do you have in your inbox right now? 10? 100? 1000? More?

The majority of IT business owners I've worked with use their email inbox as some kind of To-Do list. A very badly organised, dictated-to-you-by-others To-Do list that is forever growing.

As you've probably realised by now, using email in this way is a mistake. Using your inbox in this way – even if you flag messages for follow-up or star them as reminders – is a recipe for chaos and disaster. At best, you'll have to scroll through emails with all manner of subject lines (with likely none of them using "doing" statements that describe what action is required) to find what you need to be done, and at worst you'll just look at the long list of demands on your time and throw your hands up in the air in despair.

One of the poor habits people get into with email is reading an email, then moving to the next email. I understand why we do this – we get a tiny thrill of excitement when we receive an email, then inevitably become disappointed when we open it and the email isn't as exciting as we'd hoped. So we move on to read the next email, and get disappointed again. And the next email, and so on until we've run out of new emails to open. Then all we're left with is a load of old emails we don't really want to open again because we already know they are boring or asking us to do something when we're already busy!

Your email inbox is not a To-Do list. When email arrives you should read that email just once and then decide to do one of four things with it:

1. Delete it
2. File it away for future reference
3. Defer it to do it later
4. Do it immediately

Delete it

If an email arrives and it's of zero interest to you and never will be –

delete it. Better still, if it's a newsletter or some other form of mailing list, unsubscribe yourself and revel in the fact that you've just saved yourself time in the future having to delete another of the same type of email!

File it away for future reference

If the email isn't asking anything of you, but contains information that is of interest to you – file it away for future reference.

Some people (myself included) enjoy building folder structures outside the inbox for us to archive reference emails away into. I have a folder called "Reference" with subfolders underneath for clients, suppliers, prospects and partners – each subfolder has the company or individual's name on it. I also have a folder called "Online Orders" with separate subfolders for those businesses or organisations I buy from online. Quite honestly, with search facilities in email and web-mail applications being so good nowadays, you probably don't need folders anymore – but if you prefer the belt and braces approach (which I do) then folders might work for you.

Either way, leaving emails in your inbox for future reference is **not** the way forward. Doing so will clutter your inbox and confuse your future efforts at staying organised. Archive those reference emails out of the inbox and away.

Defer it or do it immediately

As a rule of thumb, if you read an email and it can be dealt with there and then, in under two minutes – be like Nike and just do it.

But if you read an email and it will take longer than two minutes to complete, you are unsure how to proceed, or it needs further research to respond to, defer it either to your To-Do list or calendar.

A common mistake when processing email is believing that any task created as a result of an email needs to be dealt with there and then. Attempting to follow this line of thinking is pure folly and is a sure-fire way to ensure other people are dictating your day to you.

Again, if you can't complete an email task in under two minutes then defer it. If it's something that needs doing by a certain date in the future (Send a report by 12th February), input this task onto your To-Do list with a "Due By" date.

If it's something that needs doing ON a certain date in the future (Telephone Mom to wish her a happy birthday on 12th February) then pop it onto your calendar with a reminder set for the day itself.

Whenever deferring tasks, remember to use "doing" statements. So instead of "Client Report", set the task as "Send Ajax Company Their Client Report".

If you're using Microsoft Outlook or some web-based tools, you can actually drag and drop emails directly to your calendar or To-Do list. If you do this, make sure to change the title of the calendar or task entry from the subject of the email you've received (which is often inaccurate or non-descriptive) into a "doing" statement.

Inbox Zero

Using this method of deleting, filing, deferring to a calendar or task list, or doing right there and then, many people can quickly and easily process all their new emails in a short period of time.

You can use this method to process not just new emails that have arrived, but old emails that you've already read but are still sitting in your inbox. If you've got a hundred old emails in your inbox, process those old emails ten at a time and within a few days (well, ten days to be exact!) you'll have the mythical Inbox Zero. Processing new emails using this method will mean you stay that way.

If you have hundreds or even thousands of emails in your inbox, perversely the job of reaching Inbox Zero actually becomes easier still. Why? Because those hundreds or thousands of old emails are less likely to be important at all! It'll take some time, granted, but you can quickly move through hundreds of emails that can be deleted or archived very quickly. It may help to use your email application's search facility to batch process emails – highlight all emails from a certain client and drag and drop them to a folder, for instance, or highlight all instances of a certain email newsletter and delete them in one fell swoop. Either way, it may take a bit of time and effort, but once you've emptied your inbox you'll feel a sense of peace and control – anything that needs doing is now on your calendar or in your To-Do list, not lurking in a bloated inbox!

Once the inbox is processed – both now and each day every day from now onwards – you then turn your attention to your To-Do list to decide what you want to do next. The inbox is a temporary holding position for new information. You read the contents of your inbox, assimilate new information, process it to zero and then decide what is most important for you to work on.

Further Reading

- Getting Things Done (2015 Revised Edition) by David Allen – http://tubb.co/GTDRevised

Filtering email effectively

We've looked at how to process email effectively – delete, file, defer or just do it. Once you build the habit of processing email in this way, you'll start to spot trends in the email you receive and how you process it.

For instance, we've already touched upon those emails you continuously delete without reading – perhaps email newsletter subscriptions that you were once interested in, but find no value in now. The answer here is to unsubscribe yourself from this list.

But what about those other categories of emails – perhaps the email newsletter that you do get value from, but you don't want cluttering up your inbox? Or what about emails from your friends or family that you'd love to read and respond to, but which are, in reality, low priority against your client emails?

Spotting these trends and using tools to automatically filter these emails as you receive them is a powerful way to process your email faster.

Email client filters

If you're using Microsoft Outlook, Google Mail or just about any other email client worth its salt, then the ability to filter emails either at the server level (before they hit your inbox) or the client level (as they hit your inbox) is easy.

Implementing these filters (or rules, as Microsoft calls them) should be looked at as a task you do over time, rather than completing in one sitting. Quite simply, the next time you receive an email – such as an email newsletter – that you want to read but is low priority, right click on the message and select the filter/rule option. You can filter by sender, by subject line (useful for mailing lists) or any combination of options. Set up the filter to automatically move the email into one of the subfolders we setup earlier in this chapter.

The result of setting up a filter is that the next time one of these low priority emails arrives, it is automatically moved away from your inbox – reducing the clutter and making sure your inbox is reserved for important emails – and into a subfolder where you can read it at your leisure.

Of course, using this method you have to remember to actually visit the subfolder and read those types of emails! The interesting thing here is if you forget to read these emails for a while and don't miss anything important, you'll start to question whether you need to read them at all. Another candidate for the unsubscribe list!

Again, don't try to set up all your filters in one sitting. Instead, incorporate creating filters into your regular sweep of your inbox and incrementally implement the filters that work for you. In a matter of weeks you'll find most of the work of managing your inbox is done for you, and you rarely need to create new filters.

Going beyond email client filters

When you've set up your email client filters and as the concept of filtering your emails to make managing your inbox becomes comfortable to you, you may consider investigating some third party add-ons for your email that take the concept of filtering and super-charges it.

Sanebox

One of my favourite filter tools is SaneBox (http://sanebox.com/t/2bo90). SaneBox works with Microsoft Outlook, Google Apps and a whole heap of other providers. It's a paid-for service that, once set up with your own email account, automatically intelligently filters your emails into subfolders of your choice.

For instance, you might choose to implement the @SaneNews folder. Any email newsletters you receive will automatically be redirected away from your inbox and to this folder, which you can browse and read at your leisure.

Or you may set up the @SaneLater folder. This automatically moves emails which it knows (oh, trust me, it knows!) aren't as important to you, and moves them into a secondary inbox – @SaneLater – for low priority emails.

SaneBox has a lot of other features you will find useful – including the @SaneBlackHole feature for both spammers and those people who just won't take the hint and continue to send you useless emails – and if you get nervous you can view your inbox in the old fashioned way at any time.

The best part? While you can "train" SaneBox to know which emails belong where, it does a fine job of guessing this for you based on your past and ongoing email usage – reducing the need for you to set up new filters at all.

I'd recommend taking advantage of SaneBox's two week free trial at http://sanebox.com/t/2bo90 – if, like me, you're nervous of handing your precious inbox over to a computer to manage, then don't be. SaneBox will transform the way you manage your email.

Unroll.me

As we've looked at email throughout this chapter, the topic of email newsletters has arisen a few times. Many of us subscribe to too many email newsletters, but hardly any of us actually read as many as we want to. Perhaps it's because in the modern information age we're worried about missing out on a nugget of information.

If you don't manage those email newsletter subscriptions effectively – and unsubscribing from any you don't read regularly is the best way! – they can soon overtake your inbox and distract you from the real tasks at hand.

We've already looked at how you can use email client filters and third party tools such as SaneBox to redirect newsletters away from your inbox and into subfolders.

Another third party tool, Unroll.me (https://unroll.me/) goes a step further and captures all your email newsletters before delivering them to you in a daily digest that looks a lot like a newspaper.

After creating a free Unroll.me account and connecting it to your email – it works with Google Apps, Outlook.com, Yahoo Mail and others – Unroll.me goes away and analyses all the email newsletters you receive. After a day or so of letting Unroll.me learn how you work, instead of receiving half a dozen emails – each from a different newsletter – you receive one Unroll.me digest email (your daily roll-up) each day that shows you the newsletters it's captured and allows you to view them online.

The Unroll.me tool also keeps a look-out for new newsletter subscriptions and prompts you to add them to you daily roll-up too. It's also powerful in that it allows you to easily unsubscribe from those newsletters you never consented to receive in the first place – doing all the work of nuking your subscription in the background.

Unroll.me is a surprisingly effective way to group your email newsletters together and if you become nervous you're missing anything, all those original email newsletters are still left filed away for you to find and read.

Further Reading

- Manage Outlook emails by using rules – http://tubb.co/1g9DcFK
- Using Filters in Google Mail – http://tubb.co/1lOJYXb
- SaneBox – http://sanebox.com/t/2bo90
- Unroll.me – https://unroll.me/

Responding to email more effectively

So by now we've powered up our Email-Fu by filtering our inbox – using both our email client and third party tools – so we only need to see those emails that are important to us and not be bothered by the un-important. We've also got to grips with those email newsletters that previously cluttered up our inbox.

But what if, even after we've filtered, unsubscribed, removed and managed our emails, we still feel like it takes us too long to reply to the volume of important emails we receive every day?

The solution is to get smart about how you reply to emails.

Use the telephone, not email

People assume that email is free. Email is not free. We may not pay anything to send and receive email, but we do pay in terms of the time and effort we spend on processing email.

For every email you send, you should expect one or more responses. For every email you reply to, expect more email to follow. In short, email begets email.

One simple solution is to send less email. "But," you exclaim, "when people email me, they expect a response!" Absolutely – I'm not for a moment suggesting that you become an email hermit, living amongst nature, uncontactable by civilisation. Nor am I suggesting you become an aloof email snob, only responding to email from prime ministers and royalty. No, what I'm suggesting is that if you receive an email, you resist the urge to instantly click reply and consider how best to respond to that email.

We've already looked at the fact that people can become lazy through email. They don't use email well. Rather than talking to colleagues 10 yards away, people will email them instead. They send rambling emails with dozens of questions you struggle to read properly, let alone reply to. While you can't change the habits of those who email you, you can change the way you respond to them.

The next time you receive an email from a client, colleague, prospect or peer that requires a response from you, consider picking up the telephone and calling them.

At first glance this may seem an inefficient way of dealing with an email. Doesn't a telephone call take longer to make than knocking out a quick email reply?

Possibly. But email begets email. Quite often a telephone call will allow you to quickly convey an answer, and just as quickly deal with any follow-up questions – which, in my experience, happens with most "simple" or "quick question" emails you ever receive.

By using the telephone instead of email, you'll also find you build better relationships with people. It's now (sadly) considered remarkable to pick up the telephone and talk to a human being instead of emailing them. It's therefore unremarkably easy to be remarkable, just by using telephone instead of email! You'd be surprised what an impact a quick telephone call can make over an email.

It also educates the person you're calling that email may not always be the best tool for them to use. Phrases such as "I got your email, and it seemed quicker to call you than email you back" are easy to slip into conversation, but send a powerful subconscious message to the person you are speaking to about the nature of email. You may find you end up receiving fewer emails as a result.

Of course, there are always good reasons to use email over the telephone. You and a contact are in different countries or time zones, for instance. Even then, consider whether you can fire an email back saying "I'll give you a call about this tomorrow at X". Add the call to your @Calls list along with a timed reminder for when you're both in the office, and make the call. It could save you time.

The bottom line here is that email is NOT a good tool for conversations. It's almost always quicker and easier to pick up the telephone instead. Just because you've received an email doesn't mean you need to reply by email. Try it, you may find it works!

Using Canned Responses

You probably receive a lot of email asking similar questions or making very similar requests of you. "Can we schedule a call to discuss this?", "I need to send you something by post; what is your address?", "I'm considering buying a new laptop; what would you recommend?"

Of course, as an IT business owner a common email to receive is a request for support from a client. You've probably typed out emails directing clients to your service desk email address and telephone number more times than you care to guess at!

As it stands, you probably reply to these types of emails individually – again and again. You can save yourself time and speed up your replies by using simple canned responses.

Canned responses are templates of text that you can quickly and easily paste into replies to reduce the amount of typing you have to do.

If you're a Google Mail user, then canned responses are a superb built-in function. Next time you reply to an email with an answer you suspect you'll use again, highlight the text response, click on the

"More Options" button and save it as a canned response. The next time you need to reply to a similar query by email, select a saved canned response and insert the appropriate reply.

If you're an Outlook user, then you have a similar function in the "Quick Parts" section. Save common responses as "Quick Parts" and then insert them into emails as needed.

There are also a raft of third party tools that allow you to quickly insert text into emails based on key combinations or shortcuts. Such tools allow you to cut the time you spend responding to emails drastically.

Even if the canned responses you insert aren't exact fits for the replies you need to give, you'll probably find you can customise the text much quicker and more easily than typing a new reply from scratch

Further Reading

- My experiment in using the telephone instead of email http://tubb.co/1lOPcCf
- Getting started with canned responses in Gmail – http://www.cnet.com/uk/how-to/getting-started-with-canned-responses-in-gmail/
- PhraseExpress – http://www.phraseexpress.com/

Chapter 3: How to make sure you never become overwhelmed again

By now I hope you're feeling as though you've gotten out from under the mass of tasks that were bouncing around in your head, and that you've tamed your once wild inbox.

We've also looked at strategies to help keep you organised (and sane!) on an ongoing basis.

We're all set then, right?

We would be, but sometimes we self-sabotage our own success. We know what we should do, but don't do it. Author and speaker Larry Winget shares: "Stress comes from knowing what is right and doing what is wrong."

To help you from slipping back into bad habits that might threaten to derail your success as an IT business owner, here are some strategies to ensure you never become overwhelmed again.

Create a NOT to do list

We're all very comfortable with the idea of a To-Do list – but how many of us have considered putting together a NOT to do list? A list of things that we shouldn't do each day?

It's a surprisingly powerful concept!

If you're anything like me, then while you find it relatively easily to work on building positive habits, the real challenge comes from stopping the negative habits you have. This is where a NOT to do list can help.

We've already spoken about the importance of not checking email before you've worked on an important task each day. You know it's the right thing to do, but do you do it? The first item on your own NOT to do list might be "Do NOT check email until I've completed an important task."

We also now understand that feeding our bad habit of constantly checking email is also the wrong thing to do. Have we stopped doing this? Perhaps you need to add "Do NOT check email more than twice per day" to your own NOT to do list.

Sit down with a sheet of A4 paper and scribble down anything and everything you can think of that you might consider a bad habit. Many of these bad habits are probably work related, but don't restrict your list to work alone – have a think about what you do when you get home. Do you slump on the sofa and watch TV when you know that sitting with a cup of green tea and reading a book to unwind would be healthier? Adding "Do NOT watch TV when I come home from work" might be on your NOT to do list.

To help you get started on your own NOT to do list, here's a sample of my own personal NOT to do list:

- Do NOT check my email until I've completed an important task
- Do NOT check my email more than twice per day
- Do NOT look at Twitter more than once an hour
- Do NOT look at Facebook until after work
- Do NOT eat my lunch at my desk
- Do NOT schedule meetings back-to-back
- Do NOT put my smartphone next to my bed at night

This is probably the easiest list you'll ever have to put together. Don't be too hard on yourself here, as just like with a To-Do list, having a NOT to do list with too many items means you end up being overwhelmed. Try to focus on the few things that you know you shouldn't be doing, and concentrate on them.

When you're finished, print off a few copies of your NOT to do list and strategically place them where you'll see them every day. Above your monitor at your work desk. On the fridge door in your kitchen. Anywhere where you will see it, and often.

While you shouldn't expect to eliminate bad habits in a day, or perhaps even a week, the fact that you're consciously aware of what you're doing that causes stress in your life will mean you start to question why you are doing it at all. It's my experience that after a month or so, you'll have built positive habits of NOT doing these things – freeing up your time and energy to do things that will serve you better.

Further Reading

- Why you should create a NOT to do list
  http://tubb.co/1GpY0Ta

Learning to say no

There is an old phrase "If you want something done, ask a busy person to do it." There's good logic behind this phrase! Most people who appear to be busy also appear to be achievers – the people who get things done and are always moving forwards. By asking this type of person to help you get something done, it's likely to get done! You're probably one of those busy people, and you're probably also familiar with frequently being asked to do things by people, and to do people favours.

But you're probably also familiar with that sinking feeling that comes when you're asked for something. During the time you're asked, you're mentally thinking through all the things you're already committed to doing and how you already feel overwhelmed. Despite all this, you're a people person and you find yourself saying "Yes, I'll help!" when you really wanted to say no.

Most of us find it difficult to say "No". Perhaps we don't want to feel as though we are letting down the person who is asking. Or we can't resist that desire to please others and be seen as a helpful person. Of course, many times it's entirely appropriate that we say yes – but for most of us, we know we say "Yes" when we really mean "No".

As an IT business owner, knowing how to say no graciously is a key skill to acquire. It will help you from becoming overwhelmingly busy. It will help you to avoid working with those clients and people you know you aren't a good fit to work with. And it will help you stay committed to the things and people in your life that are important to you.

Let's take an example of somebody asking you to do something you don't really want to do. Perhaps they ask you to join a project that you aren't really interested in, that you don't have time to commit to, or both.

The common response you might give here is "Sorry, I haven't got time." The trouble with this response is, as you are probably aware, you're giving the other person an opportunity to try to cajole you into saying yes – in this case stating that you don't have enough time. "I promise it won't take very long! Won't you reconsider? Please?" Before you know it, you've ended up saying yes and are now committed to doing something you didn't want to do.

The next time such a situation occurs and you're asked to do something you don't want to do, resist the urge to make an excuse and instead simply say, "Thanks for thinking of me. While it's not something I'd like to do, I do appreciate you thinking of me."

The person may follow up with an "Oh go on, please?" or something similar. Simply reiterate: "I'd rather not, but thanks for thinking of me."

The key here is not to make an excuse for saying no. If you make an excuse for saying no, you're giving the other person an objection that they'll attempt to overcome. Think about the last time you received one of those annoying cold calls selling you double-glazing when you were just about to sit down to dinner. You politely decline the caller offering you half-price double glazing by stating, "Thanks, but I don't have the money." Before you know it, the salesman is trying to overcome your objection with promises of discounts, finance and great deals. Next time they call simply say: "I'm not interested, but thanks for the call," followed by "It's not for me, but thanks for calling." You may be surprised at the results (and how warm your dinner still is).

Learning to say no is critical to ensuring that your days, weeks and months are spent focusing on what is important to you – not being drawn into things that are important to everyone else.

Further Reading

- The value in learning to say no http://tubb.co/1MeLX3g
- Saying "No" graciously http://tubb.co/1MeM1jo
- What happens when you try to please everybody http://tubb.co/1MeM4f2

Building strategic alliances

We've already looked at things you shouldn't do – your NOT to do list – as well as learning to say no. Let's continue that theme of focusing on what is important to us and not being distracted and tackle one of the most common scenarios an IT business owner is faced with.

Consider the situation. Your IT business focuses on providing managed support for small business IT infrastructures. You're very good at it and can resolve most server, workstation or network issues within no time at all. You also know how to keep your clients' networks running smoothly. In fact, you're probably a master of maintenance and monitoring. Then a client approaches you and says: "We need a new website putting together. Can you help us with that?" Despite the fact you're NOT a web developer, nor really have an interest in website design, you don't want to let your client down and you find yourself inexplicably saying: "Yes, we can do that for you."

If you're nodding your head in agreement at this scenario, then please understand that this is one of the most common mistakes I see IT business owners making – trying to be a jack of all trades, and a master of none.

By saying yes to work that is outside your core competency or even beyond your area of interest, you are doing both yourself and the client a disservice.

"But..." I hear you say, "I don't want to let the client down." I understand. "And..." you go on, "think of the money!" While I could write about how, by taking such a job on, you'll be letting the client down by trying to do a job you're not experienced enough to do, or how the job will probably be unprofitable for you and frustrating for the client, I'll simply offer this – there's a solution that means you can help your client as well as make money, all without having to do the job yourself. It's called 'building strategic alliances'.

What is a strategic alliance?

A strategic alliance is simply a relationship you build with a fellow IT business that provides products or services that are complementary to your own. In our example, if you're a managed support provider for small business IT infrastructures then some of your typical strategic alliance partners might be:

- Web designers
- Hosting companies
- CRM consultants
- SEO consultants
- Data cablers
- Telecomms companies
- Internet service providers
- Laptop repair companies

... and the list goes on. Any company that might provide a service that your clients may benefit from, but which you don't have the expertise or inclination to provide yourself.

Now, I'm not for a minute saying that you restrict your area of expertise to a narrow niche – although there are certainly many benefits from doing that. What I am saying is that moving into other areas of expertise should be a conscious decision that you make with a plan, not as a knee-jerk reaction to a client request. So if you want to start offering websites to clients get trained up, understand how to do this effectively and profitably, and start offering websites as a service to clients. But if you know little or nothing, or worse, think "How hard can it be?" when a client asks you to build them a website – that's when you need to turn to a strategic alliance partner.

How to build partnerships

You can start building relationships immediately. The next time you go to a business networking event, rather than avoid those other IT businesses in the room you may feel are competitors, approach them and understand where their area of expertise is. It's true that some of the services they offer might compete with your own – but it's my experience that most IT companies try to do too many things unsuccessfully. Delve a little deeper and understand what work they are truly qualified to do and enjoy doing. If it's something you don't do, or don't want to do, they may be a good fit to be a strategic alliance partner.

Then, of course, there are plenty of other IT businesses out there who are mature enough to know what they are very good at, and stick to it. These businesses will acquire a reputation for excellence. The next time you go to an IT user group, peer group or business networking event try asking someone in a similar field who they'd recommend for a certain discipline you'd like to build a partnership with. "Who would you recommend for building websites?", "Who would you recommend to do data cabling?", "Who do you know who is good at doing SEO?" Then ask for introductions to these recommended suppliers.

Introduce yourself to them in an open and honest way. "Hi, we focus on providing managed support for small business IT infrastructures. It's all we do and we're quite good at it, but our clients frequently ask us for advice on web design/data cabling/SEO. We'd love to partner with somebody who we can refer this work on to. Do you think that might be you?"

By being upfront about what you're looking to achieve, you'll overcome the inbuilt suspicion that occurs when one IT business approaches another. They may have thought of you as a competitor before, but you're clearly stating that you don't intend to tread on their toes and you'd like to explore the potential of actually offering them work! Few will decline such a request!

How do I create a partnership agreement?

Once you've found a fellow IT business who you feel may be a good partner for you, you need to set an expectation around how the new relationship will work.

The first way is to suggest that the next time one of your clients needs the services of your new partner, you speak with them directly, outlining the client's requirements, obtaining a quote and then, if the client is agreeable, for your partner to deliver the work under your name and banner. Any queries the client has will come through you. Your partner will bill you for any work they undertake, and you will, in turn, bill your client – perhaps adding a mark-up to cover the costs of managing the partner.

Many IT businesses prefer this method because they believe it helps them retain 'control' of the client. I understand that way of thinking, but remember that you are utilising a partner because of their expertise in an area you don't know.

With that in mind, the second way to introduce a partner to your client is to be upfront and honest with that client when they ask you to do something outside your core competency. When asked "Can you do us a website?" you might respond: "That's not something we do, but I can introduce you directly to somebody we highly recommend and who has done great work for some of our other clients."

By introducing your partner directly to your client, you're allowing the client to gain the full benefit of their expertise directly. The business arrangement will be between the client and the partner.

Don't worry about 'losing' the client – any partner worth their salt will realise the folly of trying to 'steal' a single client, as they'd miss out on future referrals from you. Also don't worry about losing credibility with the client. They'll appreciate your upfront honesty and will be grateful for the introduction to an expert in the area they are seeking. When the job is done, and done well, they'll thank you and give you credit for your part in it – and all you did was introduce them to someone else!

If you're worried about losing income from passing up a job, then you may come to an arrangement with the partner who you're referring business to. They may pay you a finder's fee or a cut of the final invoice as a thank you. But also consider sharing such referrals with no financial strings attached. It's very likely that by referring work this way, your new partner will look for ways to reciprocate and refer work YOU are an expert in back to you!

Of course, partnerships are built on trust. You may want to do thorough due diligence and even consider referring small pieces of work to your partners before you recommend them to your favourite clients. Remember, even though your partner will be undertaking the work, in part it is your reputation on the line – you are the one who made the introduction.

Done correctly though, building such strategic alliance partnerships allows your business to focus on doing what you do best – and most profitably.

Further Reading

- Why building strategic alliances can help your MSP business http://tubb.co/1MeLMF0
- How to structure a strategic alliance http://tubb.co/1MeLQoe

Outsourcing work

One of the biggest challenges of being an IT business owner is wearing dozens of hats at the same time – senior technician, marketer, the HR department, accountant, admin assistant and chief pot washer too. While all of these tasks need to be done, it's easy to fall into the trap of believing you are the person who needs to do them.

"But..." I hear you exclaim, "I'm not ready to employ a salesman, marketing head or admin assistant yet." I understand, and if you employ our next technique for staying organised, you may never need to.

Outsourcing the jobs you either don't have the time to do or, just as importantly, don't have the inclination to do, is a powerful way of freeing up your time and energy to do the things you're good at and can generate the most revenue through doing.

For example, most of us don't relish the administrative work that running an IT business generates. But that admin needs doing, all the same. While you may not be ready to hire a full time admin assistant – either there's not enough work to keep them busy, or you simply can't afford to just yet – you can outsource the regular admin tasks that eat up your time and energy to a virtual administrator (VA).

You'll notice that I mentioned time and **energy**. Energy is an important factor when considering what you should be doing, and what you should be delegating.

Here's an example from my own life as an IT business owner back in the days when I was the sole technician, dealing with support calls as well as client infrastructure maintenance and monitoring. Each morning I'd come into the office full of energy, and begin to tackle the failed client site backups, patches that needed installation, and upgrades that needed performing. By 10am I'd done that work – and felt absolutely drained. I plodded on each day, but did I have the enthusiasm to make sales calls or execute marketing campaigns – even though they were vitally important to the growth of my business? Absolutely not. I was ground down by the repetitive tasks I needed to undertake every day, all the inspiration being sucked out of me before the day had even begun.

One day, I noticed this and took steps to outsource the task of maintenance and upgrades for my client networks to a business that specialised in working with IT businesses in this way. Within weeks I had regained my energy and my mojo and made sales calls and executed marketing campaigns that saw my business win new clients. The cost of outsourcing this work was minor, and recouped in new business in no time at all.

If that story rings at all true with you, then I'd encourage you to look around your own business. What are you doing that you don't enjoy or that you don't need to do? Some examples are:

- Bookkeeping
- Daily or weekly reports
- On-site technical support
- Remote support
- Maintenance & monitoring
- Marketing
- Social media
- Website design and updates
- Cold calling
- Graphic design

... and there are many more.

Now, one of our (many) flaws as IT business owners is ego. Nearly every IT business owner struggles with letting go of jobs or responsibilities. Why? They either believe that "it's quicker to do it myself" or "nobody else can do it as well as me".

I call nonsense on both of these statements.

Firstly, my experience of outsourcing any work at all is that – just as we discussed in our section on strategic alliances – the third party is usually an expert in what they do and so even if you are their equal in knowledge and experience, they can do the job as well as you, if not better.

Secondly, it's only quicker to do it yourself if you're doing that job once. I'd bet that more than 90% of the jobs you undertake right now as an IT business owner are repetitive in some way or nature. The trick here is to slow down, document or demonstrate what you're doing, and then outsource it.

What that means is next time you need to do a job, block the time out in the diary to do it. Give yourself plenty of time. As you do the job, write down the steps you take – in effect, systemise the task (more on systemisation in a later chapter). Use screenshots of the actions you take if you prefer. Better still, record a video. However you do it, demonstrate an outline of how you complete a task and make notes of the necessary information someone else would need to complete the task – website addresses, usernames and passwords, etc.

The next time that job needs doing you can outsource it to someone else, saving yourself time and energy. Sure, there is a cost associated with working with VAs or outsourced admin assistants, but as we've mentioned, the time and energy you've saved by not doing the job can be spent on doing business building activities – such as sales or marketing – or that highly paid project your client keeps asking you to do but you can't seem to find the time for.

If you don't know who to outsource jobs to, pop along to a business networking event and meet one of the multitude of people who can help you: virtual assistants, web designers, marketing consultants, HR gurus, telesales agents, bookkeepers, accountants.

Believing that nobody else can do a job as well as you, or that you're the only person who can do a job, are both massive ego trips that you need to get over. It's been my observation in business that the most successful IT business owners are the ones who surround themselves with people who can do the job as well as or better than them, freeing up their time to pursue the things they know they need to be doing. Do they feel guilty at outsourcing work? No. Do they feel inadequate that they're hiring people who are better at doing things than themselves? No. Do they kid themselves that they can't find anything to outsource? Absolutely not!

Uncovering what you can outsource

For the remainder of this week, keep a diary of the tasks that you do throughout the day. Whether it takes you 5 minutes or 50 minutes – write it down. Then, at the end of this week, take five minutes with a cup of something warm (I'd suggest green tea, but go with what you enjoy!) and look at everything you've done. Consider whether you could have either systemised that work to outsource to someone else, or whether you could simply outsource it straight away. I'm willing to bet you'd be surprised at how much stuff you're doing that you don't really need to be doing.

Further Reading

- The E-Myth Revisited – Michael Gerber – http://tubb.co/tubblog-emyth
- Snagit, screen capture software – http://www.techsmith.com/snagit.html

- Jing from Techsmith – free screenshot and screencast software – https://www.techsmith.com/jing.html
- ScreenR, instant screencasts – http://www.screenr.com/
- How outsourcing can free you up to do what you do best http://tubb.co/1SrgREd
- Chris Ducker talks staffing and delegating for tasks, roles and team building http://tubb.co/1SrgXM8

Chapter 4: How to win more clients when you keep putting off doing marketing

Ask any IT business owner what they'd like for their business in the next 12 months, and more often than not the answer would be "more clients". But ask that same business owner what they are doing about finding new clients and typically they will drop their head, nervously shuffle their feet a bit and share that "I should be doing marketing, but I don't have the time."

I've been there myself. Most of us who become IT business owners do so because we were primarily great technicians and the business built itself around us. In the early days, clients simply found me because I was good at what I did – being a technician. But as time went on, I realised two things. That finding clients through word-of-mouth wasn't enough, and that I needed to be more than a technician. I needed to start marketing myself and my business.

For an IT business owner, marketing can feel awkward. Essentially you are telling other business owners how good you are and why they should choose to work with you. Few of us are comfortable tooting our own horn – however good we might be. And if we're uncomfortable with doing something, the tendency is to procrastinate about it. "I'll just deal with these emails," "I'll just update that server," "I'll just check to see what's happening on Facebook." Does this ring any bells?

But the reality is that if you want to grow your IT business, then you do need new clients, and to find new clients you do need to market your business. You need a marketing plan.

Before you freak out at the idea of something as big and scary as a marketing plan though, let me be really clear about what we're going to achieve in this next chapter.

You're not going to go from zero to a hundred miles per hour – from doing no marketing to becoming a marketing machine.

You're not going to force yourself into becoming a marketing braggart, shouting from the rooftops about how great you are and persuading people to buy your services.

What you are going to do is to carve out some time each week to take some small but very important steps that will start to generate interest in your IT business. Plus, these steps won't even feel uncomfortable – because you'll have a clear plan of what you need to do.

Why consistency equals success

There is an old phrase that every IT business owner should become familiar with: "Vision without execution is hallucination."

In simple terms that means that if you know that doing marketing will help you find new clients, but don't actually do any marketing, then you're not going to find any new clients. Simple, huh?

"But..." I hear you plead, "I've tried telemarketing and it didn't work for us!" or "I've tried business networking and it didn't work for us," or "I've tried direct mail/SEO/email marketing/strategic alliances/referrals and it didn't work for us!"

I hear you. So before you dismiss everything you've tried before as not working for your business, let me introduce another phrase that you should also become familiar with: "What can be measured can be managed." Put simply, if you keep track of the activities you are undertaking with your marketing, then you can see – in black and white – whether you're doing them properly and what results you are actually seeing.

It's easy to kid ourselves that we've tried a marketing activity such as telemarketing and it didn't work. But how many calls did you actually make? How often did you make the calls? How much information did you actually gather before you gave up?

By setting up a plan of activities for yourself and then executing them consistently and recording the results, you're making yourself accountable for getting those activities done. It's binary, a one or a zero – you either did it or you didn't. And by doing it and doing it consistently, you will see results.

This is where creating a Lead Generation Scorecard comes in.

Using a Lead Generation Scorecard

The concept is easy to follow. Fire up a spreadsheet. List one or more marketing activities that you want to undertake to help you find new clients. Every week you actually do those activities and record the results of doing them. So, for instance, if you want to attend a business networking event each week and meet three new business owners, you write that in your Lead Generation Scorecard. At the end of the week you score yourself. Did you attend the networking event? Great! Did you meet three new people? Great! You've achieved this week's marketing. Good job! Now repeat again next week.

It's worth remembering not to try to do too many activities too soon. We're not trying to go from zero to 100mph here. Do a small number of things successfully.

If this process sounds simple it's because it is. By taking small steps and holding yourself accountable for taking these small steps, you no longer have a vision of "doing" marketing – instead you're actually doing it. What's more, by consistently doing it, you can rest assured the results will come. You may attend a networking event this week and not find any new clients. In fact, I'm almost certain you won't. You might attend next week and not find any new clients. It's probably going to be the same story the week after too. But by consistently taking those baby steps, by turning up each week and meeting people, pretty soon you will meet a client – either directly at the event, or indirectly via a referral from somebody else you've met. This stuff works. It's the law of averages.

The beauty of the Lead Generation Scorecard is that there is nowhere to hide. You either execute the plan consistently and see the results, or you don't execute the plan and you don't see the results. A Lead Generation Scorecard doesn't allow you to record excuses. It'll be a lot easier and less painful for you to put a tick in the box next to an activity than to not. The scorecard doesn't care about your excuses for not doing something, it just wants you to do that something.

Before we move onto the activities that might make up your own Lead Generation Scorecard, a word of warning. While you might want to fill your own scorecard full of activities you think you SHOULD be taking, instead be realistic and fill it with activities you CAN take. That means if you're currently doing nothing at all then choose two or three activities that you realistically know you can do each day/week/month. Don't be over-ambitious. Once you've built the habit of doing a few things consistently, you can always add others.

Also, remember that this is a Lead Generation Scorecard, with the emphasis on the word 'scorecard'. This isn't a marketing plan. This isn't a document you write up with good intentions and then shove in a drawer to gather dust. This is a document that you will re-visit every single week, without fail, and record your results in. I can't stress this enough. If you run out of time and don't undertake any of the activities you'd planned to do, record a big fat zero in the scorecard. Don't fluff it and think "I'll do double next week". Record the zero. It'll encourage you to do better next week and it'll educate you that marketing is an activity you need to be thinking about every day – not as an afterthought at the end of the week when you complete your scorecard.

I'd recommend setting a recurring calendar appointment for 15 minutes every Friday morning at 9am where you will complete your Lead Generation Scorecard for the week. Friday morning is good because it's typically quieter than Monday morning, and it allows you some time to plan for the following week, book appointments, make phone calls and send emails to prepare yourself, etc.

So let's start to build your own Lead Generation Scorecard.

Building a Lead Generation Scorecard

Building a Lead Generation Scorecard doesn't need to be complicated. Simply create a new spreadsheet in Excel, Google Apps or your tool of choice.

At the top of your new spreadsheet, label four columns as:

- Activity
- How do we measure
- Goal
- Week ending

Here is a quick explanation of what those columns will contain.

The "Activity" column is where we will list the lead generation activities we'll be consistently taking to help us win new clients. We'll be looking at examples of those type of activities in a few paragraphs.

The "How do we measure" column is where you remind yourself of what success looks like for that activity – a check or measurement to help hold you accountable for getting the activity done properly. An example would be business networking. Your "How do we measure" column might indicate that success to you looks like "Attend a business networking event. Meet, exchange business cards and after the event follow up with 3 new people."

The "Goal" column is a reminder of how often we're committing to undertake that activity. Some activities will be daily, most weekly, but others monthly or even quarterly.

Finally, the "Week ending" column allows us to track the week within which we undertook those activities. Having a visible reminder of what we have done on a week-to-week basis can be a powerful way of showing us what we're achieving and what we need to work harder at achieving.

Remember, the scorecard is used to measure the activities we are taking. It's important that you update the scorecard every week – even if it's to record that you did absolutely nothing. Remember, "What can be measured can be managed". Recording your activity will give you a reality check over what you're actually achieving – not what you wish you could achieve. It allows you to adjust your course accordingly.

With that said, what type of activities might you consider committing to undertaking? Here are some ideas of lead generation activities that aren't a heavy lift, but are effective.

Effective lead generation activities

I'll start with a word of caution. Nearly all of the lead generation activities I suggest below are likely to strike you as a "good idea". You may be tempted to implement them all. Don't. Remember that our goal here is not to take our marketing from 0-100 mph overnight – rarely are such attempts successful. Our goal is to introduce a handful of new activities that can, if consistently executed, become powerful new habits for us.

I'd suggest grabbing a pen and paper and as you are reading the list of example activities below, write down the activity and then grade it twice on a scale of 1-10. The first grade is how effective you feel the activity is likely to be for your business – 10 being a "wow" and 6 being an "it might work". The second grade is how likely you are to undertake the activity, with 10 being an "I can do that!" 6 being an "I know I **could** do that," and 1 being an "I'd hate to do that".

Be honest about what you can commit to, and what you want to do, but in reality, probably won't. Cold calling is one that most of us would like to do, but probably won't – because of fear, lack of technique, or whatever other reason we can think of to procrastinate. For those activities you'd like to do, but probably won't, revisit them again in the near future. Your confidence will grow as you consistently undertake activities you do feel comfortable doing, and you start seeing the results of that consistent activity in the form of new leads.

With all that said, here are some activities you may consider.

Email newsletter

Writing an email newsletter is an effective way of staying in touch with both clients and prospects. Your email newsletter might be as simple as some short introductions inviting a reader to click through to read a further online article of interest to them – either on your own or a third party website. Or you might send out your opinion on a recent news story.

Whatever format your email newsletter takes, remember that to allow your newsletter to stand out from the volumes of email all of us now receive, you need to make the content of value to readers and make sure you send the newsletter out consistently – be it weekly or monthly.

Services such as MailChimp and Constant Contact can help you easily build lists and send out electronic newsletters. A prospect or client receiving an email newsletter from you can help keep you front of mind. I can't tell you the number of times I've sent out an email newsletter and somebody has got in touch saying, "Thanks for the newsletter, it reminded me I've been needing to call you about an opportunity."

A final note on newsletters. Don't be tempted to add people to your newsletter list without their permission, however interested you think they'll be. Do feel free to invite them to sign up and let them decide.

Speak to a strategic alliance partner

In an early chapter, we looked at the value of building strategic alliances with other IT companies. Once a relationship is established, perhaps through some work you've done together, it's easy to call upon somebody only when you need something from them. Don't be that person! Setting yourself a reminder to call a strategic alliance partner for a regular catch-up will allow you to strengthen the relationship and keep yourself front of mind with them. The call may uncover opportunities that may otherwise have gone unnoticed, or give you the opportunity to help your strategic alliance partner in another way you hadn't envisaged. You just don't know until you pick up the phone and stay in touch.

Create a client story

Cast your mind back over the past six months. Have you undertaken any work for a client that has got them out of a tough spot, helped them to save time or money, or just brought a smile to their face? Have you undertaken any projects? While most of us don't consider the work we do for clients to be "anything special", the reality is that there are lots of other businesses out there – many of them similar businesses to your clients – who are interested in how you've helped others.

Creating a client story – commonly known as a case study – is a powerful way to shine a light on the work you're doing to help your clients. Your client story should typically contain some basic elements.

- Who the client is and what they do
- What problem they were experiencing and how it was affecting them
- What they tried to fix the problem, and why they called you
- What you did to fix the problem
- The positive results the client experienced

If you're not comfortable speaking to clients to gather this type of information yourself, then when you next visit a business networking event, ask around for a copywriter who can help you.

Whether you write a client story yourself or through a copywriter, once written you can share the story on your website, via social media, with your prospects and with your existing clients – and don't be surprised when you receive a call saying "I read your client story and wondered if you could help us as we're in a similar situation..."

Send a blog post to a prospect

You probably read a lot of interesting articles online and in the press. You probably also think, "I was only speaking to so-and-so about this last week!"

The next time you read an article that relates to a conversation you've had with somebody – especially a prospect – grab a copy of the article (a URL, a photocopy of the page) and send it to them (email is good, post is better!) saying simply: "I saw this and it reminded me of our conversation. Hope you're well."

That's it. No need to ask them to contact you. No need to try the hard sell. Just stay in touch, gently, and let them know you're still thinking about them. Most of us don't do this anymore – so by doing it yourself you can be the one who stands out from the pack and becomes memorable above your competitors.

Create a press release

Done anything interesting lately? "Hmmm... I don't think so," you might say. I bet you have though! Have you taken on a new client? Have you hired any additional staff? Have you attended a conference? Spoken to an audience? Created a new product or service? Been nominated for or won an award?

All of these events, and many more besides, are worth shouting about via a press release.

We're not aiming for the Guardian or the New York Post here (although why not?) but typically, wherever we are in the world, we have a local newspaper – more often than not containing a business section.

A press release is simply a short news story that you share with newspapers and websites for the consideration of their editor. Writing one isn't difficult, but if you're uncomfortable doing so then seek out a local PR company or copywriter who can help you. Once written, you can feature the press release on your website as well as distributing it to the press.

Finding yourself in the press is a lot cheaper than buying the same advertising space, and it can raise your profile with prospective clients and existing clients alike.

Write a blog post

Every business should have their own blog. A blog allows you to become a thought leader – sharing your thoughts, your perspective and your experiences with the world. It allows others to get to know you, to understand who you and your business are, and it builds trust in you.

"But..." I hear you say, "who will read it?" At first, maybe nobody. Most bloggers give up when they don't get any comments, but the good ones stick at it. Remember, our lead generation activities are all about consistency.

But it's not just about people reading your blog. Just the act of writing will help you improve. Writing a blog will help you to become a better salesman, a better business leader, a better business networker, a better public speaker, even a better guest at parties! It will help you to express your thoughts and ideas better.

As Seth Peters, master blogger and businessman once said, "If you're good at it, people will read it. If you're not good at it, and you stick with it, you'll get good at it."

Bonus – a blog isn't limited to the web. It's easy to print out a blog post and post it to someone (a prospect, a client) with a small note saying: "I thought this might be of interest."

Over time, you'll become known for your blog articles – which are helpful and informative to others. That sort of reputation as an expert often leads to opportunities you haven't yet considered.

Visit a networking event

Somebody once said, "You can be the greatest IT company in the world, but if nobody knows about you, you'll never win any business!" (That somebody might have been me, just then.)

We've got a whole chapter of this book dedicated to it, but in short, attending business networking events should be an activity you're consistently undertaking.

Meeting new people at business networking events is a great way to expand your circle of contacts. It's not just about finding new clients. You might meet people who know the perfect client for you. You may meet strategic alliance partners. You may meet your next employee. But you'll never meet any of those people if you don't get out there to these business networking events.

Do a Google search (or use Bing, if you're that person I keep hearing about) for "Business Networking <your area>" – where <your area> is your city, town or district – and book yourself on to one of the dozens of business networking events you'll find. If you're not a morning person, then don't force yourself to a breakfast event – grab some lunch, or a drink after a work. It may take attending a few different events to find the one type that works for you, but it's time well spent – and experience tells me that if you consistently attend business networking events and meet new people, you can expect some interesting opportunities to fall into your lap.

Write a LinkedIn recommendation

You, like everyone else in the business world, probably use the social networking site LinkedIn.

But how well do you use LinkedIn? We'll look at LinkedIn a little later in the book in our chapter on social networking, but one often overlooked aspect is the LinkedIn recommendation.

A LinkedIn recommendation is a personally crafted testimonial that you write for someone, which then appears on their LinkedIn profile. (This is different to a LinkedIn "endorsement", where somebody glibly spends a second to click a link to indicate you're great with Windows 10, or Cisco Networking, or making a good cup of tea.)

Why is a LinkedIn recommendation useful? Well, how many people have you worked with or alongside that you had a good experience with? They may have gone out of their way to help you. You may have learned from them. You may have just enjoyed working with them. Whatever the reason, have you let them know how much you appreciate them?

A LinkedIn recommendation is a quick and easy way to let those people you do business with know how much you appreciate them. It helps forge relationships – and it doesn't take you very long.

Out of all the activities you can undertake here, writing a LinkedIn recommendation will probably take the least amount of time but give you the biggest satisfaction and do the most to strengthen your relationships. Don't be surprised if it yields unexpected benefits – such as more business flowing your way.

Send a thank you card

When was the last time you received a handwritten note or a thank you card in the post? I'm fortunate enough to infrequently receive them from clients and business colleagues to thank me for something I've done for them – some work or an introduction I've made – and every time I receive one, I find it remarkable.

Why? Because hardly anybody sends a handwritten note anymore. Everybody relies on email to say thank you or worse, assumes the other person knows they are appreciated. They might do, but then they may not, so making sure you let them know is a powerful way to build a relationship.

Cast your mind back over the past month. Is there anybody who has done you a favour, done some great work for you, or gone out of their way to help you? Let them know by sending them a thank you card, a handwritten note or a small gift. I guarantee you it'll be appreciated.

It's worth remembering that relationships are a little bit like a bank account. You have to make deposits in them before you can make withdrawals. Giving without expectation is one way to make a deposit in your business relationships, and saying thank you is another.

Write a white paper

You've probably read a white paper, even if you've not realised it. A white paper is a document that acts as a guide, exploring a certain topic or subject – typically a problem – and helping the reader understand how to solve that problem.

Do you have any problems that you consistently solve for your clients? If so, they may make an excellent white paper.

"How to protect yourself from spam" may be a white paper. "The essentials of backup and disaster recovery" may be another. And there are dozens more.

A white paper doesn't have to be lengthy – it just needs to be valuable. Don't withhold any tips or tricks because you're fearful of giving too much away – most people who read white papers do so to understand the problem, not implement the solution. They're happy to let others do that for them.

A white paper makes a handy resource to give away for free on your website or via social media. It can also be a good way of gaining permission to send someone your email newsletter. "Sign up for our newsletter and get a free white paper!" for instance.

If you feel uncomfortable about writing a white paper, don't be. Go and search for a white paper on any subject you can think of, and have a look at how it's laid out. Replicate this yourself. Or if you feel really uncomfortable about writing it yourself, hire a copywriter to put it together for you.

If you commit to writing a white paper, say, every month, after a year you will have twelve white papers that cover most of the products or services that you typically sell. These white papers will generate interest in you and your business. They'll help you build a prospect list. They'll establish you as an expert and they make great sales support materials to email and post to prospective clients. In short, a white paper is an essential tool for your lead generation activities.

Deliver a presentation

You're an expert at what you do – and your clients, and probably your friends and family, view you that way too.

How then can you persuade those who don't know you that you're an expert? Well, think about the last time you watched somebody present on a topic. I'm willing to bet that without even thinking about it, you considered that person an expert in whatever they were talking about just by the fact they were standing up talking and a room of people were listening to what they had to say!

Public speaking is most people's biggest fear. It's certainly high up on my list of fears. But there are few other ways of establishing yourself as an expert in the eyes of those who have never met you before.

Look for opportunities to present to others – business networking events are usually a great opportunity here, as most business networking groups offer slots to speakers who can educate the group on a certain topic.

Your presentation doesn't have to be slick. It doesn't have to be polished. It doesn't have to be delivered to a room full of people. You just have to know the subject you're speaking on, and talk about it. I've delivered some awful presentations over the years and I can say with experience that after even the most awful presentations I've delivered, without fail, somebody in the audience has approached me to say thank you and to enquire about learning more about working with me.

For most people, speaking in public will be the item on this list of activities that they know will deliver the most benefit, but is the one they are most uncomfortable doing. To that I say: try it! You might find you're good at it – and don't be surprised when you start to get treated as an expert by new people.

Curate content on social media

We'll take a much more in-depth look at social media in a later chapter in this book, but if social media is something you know you should do, but don't have the time to do, consider committing to becoming a content curator.

Anyone who follows you on Twitter, or reads your status updates on LinkedIn or Google+, is interested in you. To grow the number of people who are interested in you, you need to provide content they are interested in. This content doesn't necessarily need to be content you've written yourself – it can be content produced by other people that you think would be of interest to your own network.

Curating content in this way is easy. You probably read a number of blogs, websites and news pages already – perhaps while you're having a cup of coffee or taking a break. Continue to do this, but the next time you read an article that's not only of interest to you, but would be of interest to your clients or your prospects – share it via your social media networks.

Your clients don't want to trawl the BBC News website, or read The Register, or subscribe to the latest Tech News – they look to you for advice and guidance, and by curating content in this way, you can become their source on social media for the news and advice that is relevant to them.

Curate content in this way consistently, and you'll find you draw others who appreciate the fact you provide them with content of value. By following you and by you providing them with value in this way, you earn their permission to occasionally talk about your own business and your own products and services. They'll listen, because they know you consistently provide value to them.

Just don't make the mistake of making it all about you. Remember that people are bombarded by enough advertising already – you won't stand out from the crowd if it's all about me, me, me, sell, sell, sell! But by curating content of value to others, and sharing it on your social networking channels, you can expect to build an audience of people who are interested in you – and your business.

Visit a client

You probably speak to your clients all the time – typically when they've got a question for you or are experiencing a problem. But how often do you call your clients to ask them how they are? For most of us, the answer is "Not very often".

Our lead generation plan is not just about finding new clients, it's about making sure we develop the relationships with our existing clients. One excellent way to do this is to consistently stay in touch with your clients to see how they and their business are doing.

When I ran my own managed service provider, I used to frequently drop in to clients' offices with a box of donuts or a cake – just dropping by to let them know I appreciated their business and to see how things were.

It was rare to find a client who didn't appreciate an unsolicited visit from their IT guys bearing a cake or two, and most of the time the client would take the opportunity to chat with me about what was happening in their business. This chat allowed me to offer advice, to head off potential problems, and to keep my finger on the pulse of their business.

And, more often than not, it uncovered an opportunity I just wasn't looking for. Be it an upcoming new member of staff who would require a PC, a new printer required in the office, or even plans to relocate offices and all the work that goes into such a project – regular client visits, or even telephone calls to clients, help you stay in touch and be seen as a proactive partner to your client. For all of those reasons (and the fact that you can have a slice of the cake you take to clients too) it's worth committing to visiting clients regularly.

Executing the activities in your Lead Generation Scorecard

The list of potential activities you can build your Lead Generation Scorecard around that I've listed here is far from comprehensive. There are other activities, such as direct mail, telemarketing, vendor marketing, and much more that you'll probably grow into. But remember, the goal here isn't to develop an all singing, all dancing marketing plan – it's to get us started on some simple activities that, if executed consistently, will deliver results that we can build upon.

None of the activities I've listed are heavy lifts – they don't take a lot of time. But they do take a commitment. A commitment to actually make the time to get them done each week, and a commitment to record in your Lead Generation Scorecard what you've done (or, importantly, not done).

By choosing two or three of the activities above – or variations on them that suit you – and executing them every week, every month, every quarter, you'll see the results you want. New leads and opportunities will present themselves to you.

Further Reading

- Perseverance and consistency = success – http://www.tubblog.co.uk/blog/2013/07/04/perseverance-and-consistency-success/
- Creating a lead generation plan for Your MSP – http://www.mspbusinessmanagement.com/webinar/creating-lead-generation-plan-your-msp
- Creating an MSP Lead Generation Scorecard http://tubb.co/1MeMEJO
- Seth Godin & Tom Peters on blogging – http://www.youtube.com/watch?v=livzJTIWlmY
- MailChimp – http://eepurl.com/C0atX

Chapter 5: How to become a natural at business networking

The old adage "People do business with people they know, like and trust" is as true today as it has ever been. You can be the best IT company in the world, but if you haven't given anyone the chance to get to know, like and trust you, then you're unlikely to be fighting off multitudes of clients.

Attending business networking events is one of the most tried and tested methods for building connections and relationships with others. Every weekday, there are dozens of business networking events taking place in every town and city across the world. You don't have to look hard to find a regular networking event near you.

You may have already been to networking events in the past but perhaps gave up going to further events for one of two common reasons:

- You felt nervous walking into a room full of strangers.
- You didn't meet any potential clients.

Let's address those issues. Firstly, the very best of us become nervous when walking into a room full of people we don't know, especially one where we are then expected to reel off a polished introduction about ourselves and our business. It's awkward; it's nerve-wracking. For most of us who work in the IT industry, we'd probably prefer to stand in the corner and read emails on our smartphone than interrupt somebody else's conversation and introduce ourselves.

Secondly, when we do get the courage to introduce ourselves, the people we meet at these events typically aren't a good fit to work with our IT business anyway! They don't have an interest in IT, they don't need IT services, so why bother?

Both valid points. I've attended more business networking events than I can remember, and at every event I've ever attended I've struggled to find anyone who I think is a good client for me. All that stress and time out of the office, just to listen to other people talk about their businesses!

That said, my attitude towards business networking events changed once I realised one thing – that business networking events are not there for you to sell at!

"But..." I hear you exclaim, "if I'm not there to sell myself or my business to others, what is the point in attending at all?" Let's take a look at one strategy that might work for you.

Be the connector

The chances of attending a business networking event and bumping into someone who is the ideal client for you are slim. It's not impossible, I grant you, and serendipity does strike, but even if you meet somebody who you feel is the perfect client for you, try to look at things from their perspective. Why would they trust you enough to do business with you?

Most people attend business networking events trying to sell. Sell themselves. Sell their business. Sell the idea that they are the perfect solution to your problems. Except most of the time they don't bother to check with you to see what your problems are, let alone whether they can help you.

Don't be that person. Instead, when you attend a business networking event, use the opportunity to do something very few of us do regularly nowadays – listen.

Ask the people you meet...

- what they do in their business, then listen to their answer.
- why they chose to do that, then listen to their answer.
- who they work with as clients, then listen to their answer.
- what they enjoy about working with those clients, then listen to their answer.
- what their biggest challenge is right now, then listen to their answer.

Putting the focus on the other person is in complete contrast to the typical strategy of some people at a networking event who love to talk about their favourite subject – themselves.

By listening to who the other person is, who they work with, how they help other people, why they enjoy doing that type of work, and what they are struggling with right now, you can get to know the person you are speaking with quite well in a very short space of time. What's more, you'd be surprised at the people who go away thinking well of you, merely for taking the time to focus on and listen to them. "What a great conversation," they will say. "He really understood what I do!"

Repeat this same strategy for the next person you talk to. Ask questions about them, and listen to their answers. After repeating this process as little as a couple of times with different people at the event, you may be surprised that you notice some commonality between the people you've spoken to. The first person you meet may be from a marketing company that specialises in working with solicitors. The second person you meet may be a solicitor who wants to reach new customers. When you've finished listening to what they have to say, mention that you know somebody who may be able to help and ask them if they'd like you to introduce them. Introduce the first person to the second person, explaining what each of them does and how you think they may be a good fit to talk to one another. Make the introduction, then leave them to talk and repeat the process elsewhere.

It may be that by listening and understanding what the other person does, you realise they may be able to help one of your existing clients. Mention this to them and offer to make the introduction via a post-event follow-up.

It may also be that by listening and understanding what the other person does, you realise they may be able to help someone you met at a previous networking event. Mention this to them and offer to make that introduction via a post-event follow-up.

The most likely outcome is that you meet that person, listen to and understand what they do, and then offer to keep an eye out for people you think they may be able to help. You may end up surprising them by meeting someone at a future event and connecting them directly.

By focusing on other people and looking for opportunities to be the connector in this way, you'll find that networking events become a lot more enjoyable and without even trying, you're making yourself valuable to those around you, even if they aren't potential clients for you.

But how does all of this benefit me, you might ask?

Simply put, by listening to, by understanding and by looking for potential introductions for people, you're making yourself valuable to them. When people are valuable to us, it's human nature for us to want to try to reciprocate. Even if they were focused on themselves during that initial conversation, when you become valuable to them they'll start to focus on you. "Remind me what it is you do again?", "Who do you work with?", "Is there anybody you're looking to meet right now?" are all common responses from somebody who you've done a good turn for or made an introduction to.

Don't underestimate the human need to reciprocate. People will look to return the favour and introduce you to potential clients, and a warm referral from somebody goes a long way towards building trust – the trust you need to win new clients.

At first, you may be tempted to "keep score". To track who you make introductions for, and to wait for them to reciprocate. Don't bother. Some reciprocate sooner, others later, and others in ways you may not yet even begin to understand.

Being the connector also puts you firmly at the centre of a hub of fellow business owners. Even if they don't refer you business directly, you'll become known as the person who knows people. "Ask Dave, he seems to know everybody," they'll say. This plaudit alone opens up opportunities for you. Opportunities to introduce businesses to one another. Opportunities to expand your circle of contacts. Opportunities to get to know more people. Once you get started on being a connector, it's a self-fulfilling circle.

I can't tell you the number of opportunities that have fallen into my lap, not from the people I've met, but from the people who know the people I've met.

Don't try to sell at networking events. Instead, focus on the other person. Listen. Be the connector. Then watch how opportunities arise for you where you least expected them.

Further Reading

- 4 easy ways to work the room at an IT conference –

http://tubb.co/1e3hyUf

- How to make it look like you're a natural http://tubb.co/1jVkWkm
- The Go-Giver by Bob Burg and John David-Mann – http://tubb.co/GoGiverBook
- How to work a room by Susan RoAne – http://tubb.co/1MxVWO3
- Finding customers by networking http://tubb.co/1gF4RmU

Dealing with business cards

So you've visited the business networking event. You've focused on listening to other people and being the connector. You've come away with a handful of business cards. You drop them on your desk with good intentions to follow up, but before you know it, things have got in the way and the next business networking event has rolled around.

A few weeks later you look at your desk and you have a pile of business cards gathering dust.

If that scenario strikes a chord, then something to learn about business networking events is that the real value is not only to be found in attending the event itself, but in following up effectively with the people you've met after the event.

Scheduling time to follow up

One strategy I use is to schedule two sets of time in my diary. The first is to attend the business networking event. The second, typically scheduled within 48 hours, is an hour back at my desk where I can input the contact details of the people I've met into my system and follow up with them effectively. I've found that without scheduling this time, other stuff gets in the way and pretty soon I have a pile of business cards from people who I can barely remember meeting, who in all likelihood can't remember meeting me either.

By scheduling time in your diary to follow up effectively, the memory of who you met, what you talked about, and why you are following up with them is still fresh in your mind.

Using memory hooks

If, like me, you have the memory span of a goldfish and can't remember the people you met and exchanged business cards with just yesterday, there is a simple trick to use. When you meet the person and exchange business cards, take the time to write a couple of memory hooks on the back of that person's card.

Memory hooks might include:

- Where you met.
- What you talked about.
- What you promised to follow up with them on.

Where you met is simple; just jot down the name of the event. You might wonder why this is important, but if you're attending two or three events in a week then it definitely helps to remind you which event you met someone at.

What you talked about might be business related. Or it may be as simple as the fact you both spoke about how your sons' football teams are doing. Or a good restaurant you both ate at. Or where you've been on holiday. Whatever it is, write it down. The act of reminding yourself what you spoke about will jog your memory on who they are, and very importantly, will jog their memory on who you are when you follow up.

What you promised to follow up with them on is very important. If you said: "I know someone who would benefit from talking to you.

Would it be useful if I introduced you?" and they say "Yes," then failing to follow up with that introduction is a sure-fire way to get your new relationship off on the wrong foot. Instead, make a note on the back of their card of the action you said you'll take, and take it.

One final tip – make sure you take plenty of pens with you to these events. One isn't enough, as you'll invariably end up losing it or giving it away to someone else who in turn has forgotten their own pen (or given it away!).

Effectively following up

When you do sit down to follow up, aided by the fact you've scheduled time to do those follow-ups, and the fact you've used memory hooks to remind yourself of who they were, it's useful to follow a simple system.

The first step of a follow-up system is to input the person's business card and contact details in your address book. You could manually do this by creating a new contact record in Microsoft Outlook, Google Apps or your Customer Relationship Management (CRM) system. However, here's where technology can make life easier for you.

CamCard (https://www.camcard.com/) is a free app that utilises your smartphone to enable you to take a photograph of any business card and then automatically add the person's details to your contact list. CamCard is available for iPhone, Android, Windows Phone, Blackberry and other platforms and is remarkably reliable at reading all sorts of business cards and correctly deciphering the text on them. Use it to quickly scan in the details and remember to use the notes field in your contact list app to make a note of where you met the person, what you talked about, and any other keywords or tags of interest. When you need to pull those details up in the future, you may not remember the person's name, but you might remember what you talked about ("Sundarbon restaurant in Birmingham"), which event you met them at (Solihull Business Club), or even what they were wearing (blue suit with green shoes). By noting this in your contact app, you make retrieving their details a lot easier in the future.

Next, drop the person an email. If your initial meeting was a strong one, then a telephone call might be more appropriate, but for the vast majority of people you meet at events an email is more convenient and appropriate. The email should read something like:

"Hi <x>,

I enjoyed meeting you at <event> and chatting to you about <stuff>. I hope you found the event valuable too!

As promised, I wanted to follow up with you and send you <further information/introduction/content> – I hope you find it useful, and do get in touch with me if I can help any further.

I'm going to keep an eye out for <their ideal client> – would it be ok to make any such introductions directly to you via email?

Regards,

Joe Bloggs"

Let's analyse what we've done with this email.

Firstly, we've reminded them of which event we met at and what we talked about. We might think we're the most special person they met that day, but unless we give them a memory hook, they may be struggling to remember who we were!

Next, if we promised to follow up with them about something specific – perhaps an introduction, a link to a website, an article we discussed – we do so as promised.

Thirdly, we remind them that we listened to what they told us about their business and who they'd like to work with, and let them know we'll be looking to help them with a referral as the opportunity arises.

Now, don't expect a response to your email at this stage. Many people will be "too busy" to reply. That's ok – you don't write the email expecting a reply or indeed any favours, but those people who do value your email and want to build a relationship will take the time to reply and possibly even reciprocate by looking for introductions for you too.

Further Reading

- CamCard – https://www.camcard.com/
- 4 steps to effectively deal with b cards http://tubb.co/1TGOHYx

Connecting on social networks

The final step of making the most from a business networking event is about connecting the offline world to the online world: connecting with the people you've met on social networks.

We'll look at effectively using social networking in a later chapter, but for now, let's focus on the people we've met at our networking event.

Nowadays, people make it easy to be found online. When we are inputting the contact details of a business card from someone we've met at an event, these details often include a Twitter handle, a LinkedIn URL or a Skype ID. If so, our next step is made easy!

But even if you don't know a new contact's social networking details, they are easy to find. Plus there is a lot of value in connecting with them digitally too.

Tools such as Outlook Social Connector for Microsoft Outlook, and Rapportive for Google Mail both allow you to see people's social network accounts directly from your address book.

Here are a few ideas on how to effectively connect with people on social networks.

Connecting on LinkedIn

LinkedIn is the world's foremost business networking site. It's very rare to find someone, even the most IT illiterate or technophobic person, who isn't on LinkedIn. A quick search on most people's name and company will yield the right result.

When you connect with someone offline, it makes sense to connect with them on LinkedIn too. Why? Well, for a start, when you connect with someone on LinkedIn you each gain more visibility to the other's background, professional details and importantly, who else you are connected to.

A simple LinkedIn connection allows someone else to read your profile, understand more about what you do and who you work with, and your professional history. "I didn't realise you used to work at so-and-so. I used to work there too!" or "I had no idea you used to be a computer programmer. Can I ask your advice on something?" are two of the more common follow-ups I hear from people after I've connected with them on LinkedIn.

Then there is the real power of LinkedIn – who you are connected to, and the wider network.

"I notice you know Steve at IBM – could you introduce me?" or "I see you used to work with Joe Bloggs. Do you stay in touch with him?" are both common follow-ups once people have taken a look at who I'm connected with on LinkedIn.

We all have value in our networks; the things we've done, the skills we've acquired, the people we know. All of these things allow those people we've newly connected with to get to know us, to like and trust us – and for us to become valuable to them. You'd be crazy not to utilise those assets.

Incredibly, many people do just that. They connect with somebody on LinkedIn and never bother to read their profile. Or where they've worked before. Or who they are connected with. They merely connect with people because it's the "done thing" or because they can boast they've got 20,000 LinkedIn connections.

Don't be that person! Realise there is greater value to be had in a smaller number of strong connections than a wider number of loose connections. Don't "friend collect" on LinkedIn, but do appreciate the value a new connection can provide to you and you to them.

Finally, remember to personalise any connection requests you make on LinkedIn. Instead of sending the person the boilerplate "I'd like to add you to my professional network", make it valuable for the other person to do so. A short version of your effective follow-up email such as:

"Hi Steve,

We met at <event> where we discussed <stuff>.

I thought it might be useful if we connected via LinkedIn to help stay in touch and so you could see if any of my connections are useful to you. Take a look, and if I can introduce you to anyone of interest – please don't hesitate to ask me!

Regards,

Joe Bloggs"

This introduction helps you stand out from the pack because most people don't bother. It's also worth remembering that like any successful platform nowadays, LinkedIn is now sadly full of individuals spamming others and trying to connect so they can sell to them. The above style of non-boilerplate message helps make sure your introduction isn't ignored.

Connecting on Twitter

Many people now use the microblogging platform Twitter for business. We'll look at Twitter in greater depth in a later chapter, but for now, once you have someone's Twitter handle, it's worthwhile connecting with them.

Following a new contact on Twitter is a good way of showing the other person you want to stay in touch. They'll typically reciprocate and follow you too.

Even if you don't want to clutter up your Twitter feed by following too many people, you should always consider giving the person (and the event and the venue!) a shout-out on Twitter. For instance, tweeting the following:

"Enjoyed attending #BSMC at @THSHBirmingham today! Great to meet @KarenStrunks and @AlanMatthews11 there!"

This lets your follower know you were at the #BSMC event and because you mentioned the venue's Twitter account (in this case, @THSHBirmingham), you are more likely to get re-tweeted. This all expands your visibility.

Finally, everyone likes to be acknowledged, so by mentioning

@KarenStrunks and @AlanMatthews11 – two of the nice people you met at said event – they are likely to spot this and reciprocate, perhaps by responding, perhaps by following you, or both.

Alternatively, even a simple tweet such as *"@KarenStrunks Lovely to meet you at the Town Hall networking event in Birmingham today. I enjoyed chatting about our favourite cakes!"* is an effective way to put up your virtual hand and say to someone: "Hi, I'm here!"

Whatever you choose to do, Twitter is an effective channel for continuing the conversations you began at the business networking event. Stand out from the crowd and don't ignore it!

Other social networking platforms

Other social networking platforms might be a better fit for you.

For the majority of business people, Facebook remains the platform they use less for business and more for friends and family, so be aware of that fact before you try to "friend" someone on Facebook who you've just met at an event. Liking a person's Facebook business page might be more appropriate.

Visual sites such as YouTube, Instagram or Pinterest also allow you to connect with people who upload videos and photos. Leaving a comment on the videos they've shared or business photos they've uploaded may help build your new relationship. But be aware when uploading photos or videos of other people without asking their permission first, many of us are still uncomfortable with having our photograph taken, let alone it being shared with the world!

As with all things online, when using social networking think of the other person and how they use social networking sites themselves. If in doubt, treat with caution or ask for permission before proceeding with any friend requests or sharing images.

Further Reading

- Outlook Social Connector – http://office.microsoft.com/en-gb/outlook-help/turn-on-the-outlook-social-connector-HA102809417.aspx
- Rapportive – https://rapportive.com/
- Effectively using social networking to build your IT support business http://tubb.co/1gF4Qze
- Why I reject 25 LinkedIn connection requests per month http://tubb.co/1Sl2MIl

Chapter 6: How to use social media to win business without spending all day at the keyboard

We have already touched upon it in a previous chapter – now let's tackle the activity that most IT business owners feel they should be doing but:

a. have no idea how others find the time to do it

b. secretly have no idea WHY others are bothering to do it

I'm talking, of course, about social media.

Why use social media?

Those that actively use social media absolutely "get it" – they see the value of it, they enjoy doing it, and if they're good at it, they win business through it.

Those that don't use social media are still wondering what all the fuss is about. You have enough things to do already without sharing with an uninterested world photographs of what you're having for dinner, right?

While it's true that you probably have enough things to do already, the fact of the matter is everyone is using social media and if you aren't using it, and using it well, you're giving the rest of your market a competitive edge over your own IT business.

This isn't just a case of following the "in" crowd either. When I mean everyone is using social media, I mean the people who work for you.

The people who buy your products. The people who talk to other people about you.

One IT business owner once told me: "My clients don't use social media, so I don't need to either!" To which I responded: "What about those companies who aren't your clients? Do they use social media?" He'll never know.

For me, the top three reasons to use social media for your business are:

1. It enables you to build trust in your company and your services.
2. It enables you to establish yourself as a trusted authority.
3. It enables you to engage in conversations with those who wouldn't normally find you.

But this isn't a book all about social media, and if you're a social media naysayer then I'm not here to convince you otherwise. I'll leave that to your competitors. This chapter is for those of you who are already using social media in some form and want to leverage it to enable you to win business without spending all day at the keyboard. Here are some tips on making social media work for you.

How to be successful with social media

I'll state upfront that while I'm a big fan of social media, it is a tool like any other that you can master or be mastered by. Like email or your web browser, social media can be a big time drain if not managed properly. I'd suggest that you resist the urge to dip in and out of social media. Instead, batch your social media activities so that you are dealing with social media in the same way as you deal with email, at set times each day. The lure to "just check in" is always there, but doing so will see you waste a lot of time and effort. You have been warned!

The best way of saving time and effort with social media is to understand what works, and what doesn't.

Let's start with the most important lesson. The key to being successful with social media is not to sell.

"But..." I hear you cry, "you said we'd win business through social media!"

And you will, but only by providing value to your audience – not by hitting them over the head with a sales mallet.

Think about it. Every day, all of us are bombarded with advertising messages. TV, radio, newspapers, web adverts. And what do we do? We turn off. We filter it out. Why then would anybody follow your Twitter feed if all you do is talk about what you are selling?

Take a look at some of your competitors' Twitter feeds. If every tweet is "We're a great IT company!" or "Buy our offsite backup service!" then I'm willing to bet they have little or no followers. Why? They aren't offering anything of value – they're just shouting about themselves!

But if you offer valuable content to your audience – sharing articles, advice and guidance that helps them to get better at what they do – then they won't mind if occasionally you mention a special offer or a service you are selling.

But even if you rarely or never mention what you sell, people will ask to buy from you anyway. Why? You've provided value to them and they want more of that, so they ask you questions about how you could help them more. Oh, and they're willing to pay for it too.

The content you share doesn't even need to be yours. While posting your own blog posts and tips is great, it takes time to create this content. Thankfully, you can provide as much, if not more value, by curating content from others and sharing it with your audience.

The key to curating content from others – blog posts, news articles, help and advice – is to understand that it must be of interest to your audience, not just to you. So while you and your team might really enjoy that article on optimising your Active Directory for Exchange use, how many of your clients or prospective clients share that passion?

No – better to share articles about subjects your clients will find of value. Ten ways to market your business using technology. News articles on business growth. A help guide on reducing debtor days using electronic methods. These are the type of articles your clients will find value in, and appreciate you for.

Finally, it's not enough to take the attitude of "build it, and they will come". While sharing valuable content will attract an audience slowly but surely, it's worth remembering that social media is about conversations.

Don't always be transmitting. Look for opportunities to build a conversation. Seek out people talking about topics of interest. Share articles with them. Offer advice. Share their content. You'll find that this engagement will build an audience much faster than sitting back and waiting for them to find you.

So in conclusion, the three things to remember when you're using social media are:

1. **Don't sell** – you first need to earn permission to talk about you and your products and services.
2. **Offer valuable content** – give your audience content they find valuable and they will keep coming back to you for more.

3. **Engage in conversation** – don't always be transmitting. Look for opportunities to start and continue conversations, and add value to them.

How to use a social media management dashboard

Whether one person or a team of people is responsible for your business' social media usage, you need to be organised. One way to get and stay organised is by using a social media management dashboard.

Whether you are using LinkedIn, Twitter, Facebook – or indeed all of them – a social media management dashboard allows you to save time bouncing between different social media websites to stay up to date. It draws together all the conversations, all the status updates, all the information and all the views you want to take in a single website that you can use to quickly and efficiently manage your social media empire.

There are a number of options when it comes to picking a provider for a social media management dashboard, but my choice is Hootsuite (http://tubb.co/HS-Pro).

Hootsuite is scalable. As well as being a good fit for smaller businesses, or even one man bands (I use Hootsuite both personally and professionally, for instance), Hootsuite is used by much larger businesses who have teams of people looking after their social media. You may have one person in charge of your social media right now, but having the flexibility to easily add others – be it other employees, a virtual assistant or an external marketing company – is a featured not to be overlooked.

In a nutshell, Hootsuite collates all your social media account streams into a single website that you can view on your desktop, laptop, tablet or smartphone. There is no software download –

Hootsuite is a fully cloud-based application.

Using Hootsuite you can read, reply, write and schedule status updates across multiple platforms – all at the same time if you choose to.

Hootsuite also allows you to track conversations – and who has already replied to messages – so you don't waste time replying to something that's already been dealt with.

As your usage of social media improves, you can add analytics and track metrics to understand where your social media efforts are best targeted.

The best thing? For a single user, Hootsuite is free. For more than one user, Hootsuite's Pro version is low cost.

As mentioned, there are other social media dashboards out there – Twitter has its own tool in Tweetdeck, for instance – but Hootsuite is easy to pick up and learn, is backed by some great training videos and good support, and is free for you to start using today.

Tips on using Hootsuite

The best thing about Hootsuite is its flexibility. You can customise Hootsuite to match your own social media usage and goals. For that reason, I'd encourage you to start using Hootsuite and use Hootsuite's own training articles to bring yourself up to speed – it's time well spent.

That said, here are three tips I'd recommend you use to minimise the time you spend in Hootsuite and maximise the benefits you get from it.

Scheduling updates

We'll look at scheduling updates later in this chapter, but for now let's just say that you should drip-feed your content updates rather than push them all out in one great gush – and Hootsuite helps you do this easily.

Say you're composing a tweet in Hootsuite's "Compose Message" area. Instead of sending it now, click the little calendar icon. Select a date and a time you'd like the update to be published, then click "Schedule".

The pending tweet (along with any others) will be displayed in your "Pending Tweets" column, and will automatically be published at the date and time you specify.

Bulk scheduling

If you have a lot of status updates to share, then Hootsuite allows you to upload a spreadsheet containing those updates and the dates/times you'd like them to be published.

Bulk scheduling is a Hootsuite Pro feature – it doesn't appear in the free version – but this feature alone can save you hours of time in scheduling a marketing campaign via social media, so it's well worth being aware of.

Use streams

Hootsuite's single best feature is its ability for you to configure "streams" – which are basically columns that display a customised filtered view of social media for you.

Some streams I'd suggest you configure as an IT business using social media are:

- **Mentions** – a stream of people who mention you online – either by social media handle or by name – enabling you to respond to them.

- **Pending Tweets** – as mentioned earlier in this chapter, having a stream displaying your schedule tweets allows you to keep track of what you are posting to social media in the future
- **Sent Tweets** – It's easy to lose track of what you've already said! A "Sent Tweets" column allows you to remind yourself of what you've said and to whom.
- **Clients** – create a stream and add those of your clients who are using social media to this stream. Engaging with existing clients on Social Media – by sharing their content and responding to their updates – helps maintain a good relationship with them in the real world.
- **Prospects** – create a stream to keep track of those prospective clients who are using social media. Look for opportunities to engage – such as answering their queries, introducing them to others, or referring them to online resources they will find value in. Resist the urge to sell to them unless they specifically ask for you to.
- **Vendor Partners** – keep up to date on what your vendor partners are saying via social media. They may share special offers, training opportunities or other news of value to you. Don't forget to engage with them and share their content with your audience too – you'll become their favourite partner if you do!
- **Strategic alliance partners** – we looked at the value of strategic alliance partnerships in an earlier chapter. Keeping track of their social media activity through a Hootsuite stream and engaging with these partners is a great way to stay front of their minds.
- **Competitors** – Staying aware of what your competitors are saying and doing can give you a competitive edge. A Hootsuite stream featuring status updates your competitors

are putting out is never a bad thing.

- **Industry Experts** – You can learn a lot from listening to what the experts in the IT industry are saying. You may have one or more Hootsuite streams to follow IT experts, marketing experts, HR experts and more.
- **Tech Journalists** – Keeping your ear to the ground for the latest technology news is important. There are a swathe of tech journalists who will appreciate you reading, commenting and, importantly, sharing their latest articles. Engage with them often enough and don't be surprised if you're asked for a comment for their latest article.
- **Communities** – There are numerous benefits from engaging with your peers, from learning to collaboration opportunities. Consider adding a Hootsuite stream that features status updates from those peers you'd like to keep an eye out for.
- **Local Businesses** – Engaging with your local community is a key strategy for raising awareness of your business with the people who are most likely to buy from you – those people on your own doorstep. Seek out fellow local businesses, even those who you don't consider clients, and join in the conversation. You'd be surprised at the opportunities that fall into your lap as a result of doing so.

How to quickly curate content

We've mentioned the value in curating content that your audience will find valuable, and the fact that this content doesn't need to be of your own making. The next question is – where do we find this content?

The short answer is that you've probably already found it. If you browse technology news sites, blogs, read email newsletters or follow any social media then you're already receiving more links to valuable content than you perhaps realise.

The challenge now is to be the curator, filtering out the content that is good, relevant and valuable to your audience, and leaving the uninteresting articles behind.

The good news is, there's no need to make a special effort to do this. Continue to click on those articles that look like they are interesting, and if you think your audience would appreciate reading that article too – share it with them.

It just takes a few seconds after you've read an article to share it. Most web pages and blogs already have some form of social sharing built in – a Facebook share button, a "Tweet this" or a Google "+1" button – that makes it easy for you to share with your audience.

Build a habit of sharing content in this way and remember to give credit where credit is due. If you read an article as a result of a tweet somebody else sent out, reference that person in your tweet. You can also reference the original author or journalist in this way too. Some people hesitate to give credit to their sources, thinking that it makes them look less of an expert. For me personally, that attitude just screams of insecurity on their part. Giving credit to others is the sign of a person or business who is appreciative of those around them – who acknowledges he is part of a wider community of experts and influencers. Your clients and prospective clients will see you that way if you give credit too.

A final tip on curating content. There are days when you glance at tweets, when you briefly look at an email newsletter, when you spot an article that you think will be of interest to your audience but you don't have the time to read the article and potentially share it with your audience there and then. On these occasions, use a tool such as Pocket (http://getpocket.com/) to store the article for reading later.

Pocket is a free app for all the major platforms that plugs into your web browser and allows you to save articles with a single click to your own private "read later" library. Then, when time permits, you can visit your Pocket library and read those articles in your own time – sharing them with your audience if they are suitable.

I personally find it useful to have a Pocket "read later" library for those spots of weird time – commuting on a train, waiting in the doctor's surgery, queuing at the local store; time I'd otherwise be tempted to fritter away on Facebook or spend daydreaming. With Pocket I can instead read an article I'll find interesting, and top up my social media content curation efforts at the same time.

Drip-feeding content

Earlier in this chapter, we looked at the value of curating and sharing valuable content with your audience.

But have you ever looked at the Twitter updates from some businesses who have a single person looking after their social media? You can set your watch by when they "do" social media – they share a deluge of articles in one go, like a machine-gun firing out bullets of content one after the other. The result? While the articles that they are sharing might be valuable, you can have too much of a good thing and so readers turn off to the deluge of information.

It's far better to drip-feed content to your audience. Share an article here and there, perhaps a few times a day – leaving your audience to take bite-sized snacks of the content you're sharing, allowing them to digest in easily manageable chunks.

You could sit down and share your social media updates three or four times a day. But, as we've already seen with our social media management dashboard – Hootsuite – earlier in this chapter, there are ways to schedule your updates to be published when you're not at the keyboard. One of the best ways of doing this is with the app Buffer (http://bufferapp.com/r/bcb2f).

Buffer is a free app – with a premium version containing more features – that allows you to build a "reservoir" of pending status updates and for them to be shared when you want them to, any time of day or night.

You might decide that your particular audience reads their first tweets or Facebook updates at 9am, followed by another one around 11am, before they return from lunch at 2pm to read some more tweets, and again on the commute home at 5pm.

With Buffer, it's easy to set up a schedule to automatically send tweets out at these times during a weekday, perhaps even with a different schedule at the weekend. But unlike Hootsuite's schedule tweets, you're not scheduling a particular tweet; you're instead telling Buffer to share whatever the next tweet is in its reservoir at the scheduled time.

Buffer is available for PC, Mac, Chromebook, iOS, Android, Windows Phone and many other platforms. You can add content to your Buffer reservoir from any of these platforms, and you can even email content to your Buffer too.

The value to you here is great. You can use tools (such as Pocket, which we mentioned earlier in this chapter) to consume content, and schedule it to be shared with Buffer later on.

No more glut of updates – just a continuous drip feed of content being scheduled in the background, all of which your audience will thank you for. They may even think you spend more time at the keyboard doing social media than you actually do. Ssh. I won't tell them otherwise!

How to find conversations to engage in

In an earlier part of this chapter, I mentioned how you could set up "streams" in Hootsuite to track those people and businesses you want to follow online.

But that begs the question, how do you find people to follow in the first place?

Obviously, many of us connect with prospective clients, local businesses, industry experts and even competitors "offline" – at business networking events, peer groups, trade shows and other gatherings. It's not difficult for us to then seek out those people and find their social media profiles to stay in touch.

But what about those other people who we don't know offline? What about the people who are asking questions we can answer, or looking for services we offer? What about the people who are talking about us directly, but not talking to us directly!

There are free tools that will search for instances of phrases or keywords online, and instantly report back to you on them. This can be really useful if you want to keep a track of what is being said about you (or your competitors, or your clients) online. You could keep an eye out for a keyword or phrase – such as "IT support Birmingham"; that's typically a part of a question such as "Can anybody recommend a good IT support company in Birmingham?" – that you'd like to respond to.

The first tool is Google Alerts (www.google.com/alerts) which, once set up, continuously monitors Google search for new instances of any keyword or phrases you tell it to look for.

So you might set up Google Alerts to monitor instances of your business name and Google Alerts will email you every time it comes across a new blog post, forum posting or article that references you.

The second tool is more social media specific than Google Alerts, and is SocialOomph (www.socialoomph.com). SocialOomph has many features, some of them only available in its Premium paid version, but one of its best free features is its social media keyword monitoring feature. Once you've configured SocialOomph with the relevant keywords and phrases, it will send you an email highlighting all the instances of that keyword or phrase.

Both Google Alerts and SocialOomph offer you a powerful and free way to look for opportunities for engagement – conversations and discussions you could add value to or otherwise contribute to.

As with all search engines, both Google Alerts and SocialOomph need a little bit of trial and error. A search for "IT support" might produce thousands of hits every day, but "IT support +Birmingham" considerably less. Don't let initial floods of information overwhelm you. The web, and social media in particular, is a vast and busy place. Don't try to consume all the information it has to offer. Use filters such as Google Alerts and SocialOomph to weed out just the information and conversations you are interested in.

Further Reading

- Hootsuite Pro – http://tubb.co/HS-Pro
- Tweetdeck – https://tweetdeck.twitter.com/
- Pocket http://getpocket.com/
- Buffer – http://bufferapp.com/r/bcb2f
- Google Alerts – http://www.google.com/alerts
- SocialOomph – https://www.socialoomph.com/

Chapter 7: What to do if you think you're too small to be noticed by your vendor supplier

All IT businesses have one or more vendor suppliers whose products and services they predominantly sell. If you work within the traditional IT space, that vendor is likely to be Microsoft. If you're one of the new breed of cloud IT specialists, then that vendor might be Google. Chances are the decisions that vendor makes now and in the future will affect your IT business directly.

Yet when I ask most IT business owners what their relationship is like with their vendor suppliers, the answer I most often hear is "We don't have a relationship!"

While it may seem odd to profess to not having a relationship to speak of with the vendor whose products and services your business sells, when I press IT business owners to explain why this is, the answer I most commonly hear is "We're too small for them to care about us."

I understand this preconception. Why would a big business like Microsoft, Google, Dell or anyone else for that matter care about you as a partner? They have plenty of other big businesses who are selling much more than you ever could, right?

Well, while it's true that you may not be a vendor's biggest partner, it's entirely untrue that you can't become that vendor's *favourite* partner.

Why build a relationship with your vendor partners?

But why would you want to build a relationship with your vendors at all? Surely the relationship is as simple as you buy the vendors' wares and sell them to your customers and clients?

For most IT businesses, that simple supplier relationship may be enough. But you don't want to be most IT businesses. You want to be the best IT business – and it's my observation that the best IT businesses build relationships with their vendors. In fact, it's my experience that once you've reached a certain size with your IT business, it becomes essential to your continued growth that you have a good relationship with your vendors. Failure to build such relationships means you reach a growth plateau, working hard to maintain your size but struggling to grow further.

But for even the smallest of IT businesses, having a vendor *partner* helps your business grow faster than it could alone.

Nearly every IT business could benefit from:

- Marketing development funds
- PR opportunities
- Free products for internal use
- Preferential technical support
- Access to vendor senior management
- Opportunities to use new products ahead of competitors
- Invitations to exclusive events

But if you ask most vendors what they find most difficult about working with their partner base, they'll answer that most partners expect the world from them – but aren't prepared to offer anything in return. Think about it – if your clients asked you to over-deliver on their service, time and time again, but with no guarantee of future custom (or even a thank you!), would you want to continue working with them?

Instead, be the exception – put your vendor first. Think about how you can help *them.*

In this chapter we'll explore techniques and strategies you can use to build a relationship with your vendor suppliers – regardless of how big or small you are.

Choosing your vendor partners

Before we begin building relationships with our vendor partners, it's important to understand that, just like any set of relationships, the more of them there are, the harder to manage they become.

Many IT businesses make the mistake of opening accounts with dozens of different IT vendors, suppliers and distributors, deciding where to place their custom based on one factor alone – price.

This is understandable. For most IT businesses, the price at which they can buy products and services dictates the price they can sell those products and services to their clients. And typically, the lower the price, the better.

But if you're a vendor, knowing you're competing purely on price means you're unlikely to be motivated to offer value above and beyond the competition. After all, as the IT business owner you are only going to end up buying the cheapest – right?

Instead, give some thought to the vendors you most want to work with. For most IT businesses, you can reduce the number of vendors you need to work with into a few categories.

- Hardware vendors (Dell, HP, Lenovo, etc.)
- Software vendors (Microsoft, Google, etc.)
- Distributors (TechData, Ingram Micro, Westcoast, etc.)
- Remote monitoring and management vendors (LogicNow,

Autotask Endpoint Management, AVG, Symantec, etc.)
- Line of business vendors (Sage, Kashflow, Xero, etc.)

There may be others for your business – especially if you specialise in a certain niche – but make sure you choose one primary vendor in each category to minimise the number of vendors you are working with.

Let that vendor know that they have become your preferred supplier. Going forwards, ensuring all your business is placed with a single vendor supplier means instead of diluting your business across many vendors, never really making an impact with any one of them, you're maximising your investment in a single relationship. This step alone will make sure you appear on their radar and are noted – whatever your size – and you're likely to be treated more favourably than the vast majority of IT companies who act in a mercenary fashion, shopping on price alone.

If you'd like to start working with clients who don't just come to you because you're the cheapest but work with you because you add the most value, start building relationships with your vendor suppliers in the same way. This shift in thinking away from cost and towards value will quickly permeate your entire business.

Building a relationship with your account manager

Regardless of your size, one thing is true about the size of most vendors – they are big! It can be difficult, for instance, to build a relationship with Microsoft – one of the world's biggest software vendors. So where can you begin?

The first step to building any vendor relationship is to build a relationship with a reliable account manager. If you currently don't have an account manager, ask your vendor how you can be assigned one. Explain to them that you want to develop the relationship with them to enable you to sell more of their products or services. Few vendors will ignore this type of request – and if they do, it may be time to consider working with a different vendor.

Once you've been assigned an account manager, treat them as an ally.

Most IT businesses treat their vendor account manager as an adversary. Somebody who is constantly looking to sell to them. Somebody working on behalf of the vendor and so not working in your business' best interests.

The reality is, once you build trust with your vendor account manager, they will work on your behalf – looking for opportunities for mutual benefit, not just their own benefit. Most people building a career as a professional account manager understand why it's healthier to build a long-term relationship that is sustainable, not a short-term relationship that will quickly expire.

What are the steps you can take to treat your account manager as an ally?

Well for starters, after introducing yourself to them, explain that you've reviewed the market and as a business, have decided to make a commitment to a relationship with them. Share your business plan with them – let them know the amount of business you expect to put their way both now and in the future. In short, be open and honest with them about who you are and where you are going.

But don't focus too much on yourself. Remember that, like any new business relationship, the key to making sure you're attractive to the other person is to ensure they understand what is in it for them.

And when I say what's in it for them, I don't mean just the vendor

– I mean your account manager specifically!

Ask them questions like "Do you mind me asking how you are compensated?" or "Can I ask, how could we become YOUR favourite partner?"

Explain to your account manager that you are committed to helping THEM succeed – and one way you can do this is by understanding how THEY measure success.

You might assume that success to them is based purely on how many products or services they sell to their customers. Undoubtedly, most account managers or sales professionals are bonused on sales targets – but don't assume that this is the only thing they are interested in.

Here are some examples of how your vendor account manager might be compensated.

New Partners

If your account manager receives a bonus every time she brings a new partner on board, then offer to actively help find and introduce your peers to her.

Training and Certification

Many vendors would like their partners to train both their sales team and engineers on the products and services they sell. Some vendors have certification programmes to help distinguish the partners who have committed to high levels of competency in the use of their products and services.

Your vendor account manager may well be compensated depending on the number of engineers who undertake training or pass certifications. Why not commit to putting your engineers and salespeople through training and taking certification exams? Doing so will help improve your standing with the vendor, help your account manager reach their targets, and help your clients understand that you are committed to excellence.

Attendance at events

Most vendors put together an annual conference or other event that they'd like partners to attend. Many vendors compensate their account managers on the number of clients they bring along to these events.

Make sure you commit to attending such events, and that you schedule one-on-one time with your account manager while you are there – cementing the relationship further.

Competitions

It's not unusual for vendors to run competitions for clients, rewarding them for success in areas – typically targeted around a new product or service. Many vendors compensate their account managers dependent upon the number of their clients who get involved and the level of their involvement.

Making sure you keep the channels of communication open with your account manager will mean you're aware of these competitions and you can commit to entering them – and winning them! Doing so will reflect well on both you and your account manager.

Testimonials

While your account manager probably won't be rewarded directly for a client testimonial, they'll rarely turn down the opportunity and it may win them some kudos with their manager and the marketing department! Make the offer to your account manager to write a testimonial for the vendor to use, sharing how using their product or service helped your business.

Remember that once you've built a relationship, you can also write a

LinkedIn testimonial for your account manager to share with others about how they have helped you both achieve success. Oh, you are connected with your account manager on LinkedIn, right? Doing so helps give you both visibility over what each other is doing, helping both relationships to thrive.

And remember, there isn't an employee anywhere in the world who doesn't like to impress their boss. Consider finding out who your account manager's boss is, and let them know how valuable you find your relationship with your account manager and how it has helped your business.

Staying in touch

Finally, are you the sort of IT business owner who ducks telephone calls from your vendor account manager, worried they are trying to sell you something?

Flip the tables around and make a regular call to your account manager something that you commit to doing. Call them and let them know what you are working on – which deals you have in the pipeline and how it will impact your purchasing from them. Let them know the success you've had with their product – giving them opportunities to ask for testimonials or case studies. Ask them how they are and how you can be of help to them.

The next time you win a piece of business based on the vendor's product or service – tell them about it! The account manager will share your success with his boss, who in turn will share it with her boss. Your name will be noticed as everyone wants to be seen to be involved with a winning team!

So few IT companies would consider doing this that it will *really* make you stand out from the crowd. It's not that difficult to be remarkable – so go be remarkable!

How to ask your vendor for discounts

Going back to the start of this chapter, remember when I said that most IT businesses ask their vendors for things without offering anything in return? Nothing is truer than this when it comes to discounts.

Think about it. Have you ever had a client ask you for a discount for no other reason than, well, they don't want to pay so much? Not much of an incentive for you to lower your prices, is it?

So if you find yourself in a position where you'd like to get keener pricing on a product or service from a vendor, consider offering something in return for the favour.

For instance, many vendors offer a tiered pricing structure, where customers are rewarded with keener pricing based upon the volume of business they generate. Your business may not be doing enough volume to reach the next available tier right now, but how about if you committed to the vendor to reach that next tier within a certain time frame (the next quarter or the next year) if they offered you the next tier pricing... today. You might think this is a cheeky request, and indeed, it may be considered so, but you're effectively negotiating based on a commitment to sell more of that vendor's products or services. You might even go as far as to say you'll happily settle up the balance if you don't reach the volume you've committed to. What vendor would say no to such an offer?

In a similar vein, many cloud services are offered by vendors on a monthly basis. If you'd like to reduce your bill, asking for a discount on your monthly cost may be difficult for the vendor to agree to. But how about if you asked the vendor if they'd offer you a lower monthly bill if you committed to a long-term deal – say, 18 months or 3 years? The vendor will quite often agree to reduce your monthly bill and make less profit over a longer term, provided they have your commitment to a long-term relationship.

The bottom line is, be prepared to negotiate with your vendor by offering something in return for a discount – not just asking for a lower price with nothing offered in return. Most vendors will be happy to negotiate over cost provided there is something in it for them – be it a longer-term relationship or a commitment to an increase in volume of sales.

Chapter 8:
How to make the time to stay up to date on trends and stay ahead of the competition

One of the most challenging areas of running an IT business for any owner is the nature of the IT industry – namely, continuous change.

Change is also one of the reasons IT professionals are so in demand. From a customer's perspective, as MSPs we're not really being asked to just "fix this please", but to take responsibility and remain accountable for their technology now and into the future.

The common consensus is that the marketable half-life of any IT skill (that is to say, the amount of time your skill remains relevant and valuable) is two years. That means whatever technical skill you acquired last year, by the end of next year that skill will probably not be so relevant any more.

Any of us who took pride in passing our Microsoft Certified System Engineers (MCSE) qualification in Windows NT 4 will know this feeling all too well!

Of course, there are some skills that remain relatively evergreen – but for the most part, the IT industry is one built on constant change. As an IT business owner, not only do you need to keep your technical skills relatively sharp, but you also need to keep growing your leadership skills, you need to be cultivating relationships with vendors and understanding how their new products and services can help your clients and your business, and you need to be aware of industry news and views. In short, the learning never, ever ends.

But with your plate as an IT business owner already full to spilling over dealing with clients, employees and suppliers – how on earth do you find the time to keep up to date? In this chapter, we'll explore some strategies that, when consistently executed, will help you remain current and maintain a competitive edge over your rivals.

Surround yourself with positive, successful people

The first piece of advice I'd give to any IT business owner is to be very, very aware of the people you spend time with. The colleagues, peers and even friends you spend the majority of your time with will mould who you are as a person and your outlook in life.

We've all experienced this. That friend who, when you get together, seems to do nothing but complain about his lot in life? How do you feel when you come away from spending time together? I'll hazard a guess that you feel drained, uninspired and listless.

Contrast that with the entrepreneur you met at a business networking event for the first time. Full of energy, you were inspired by her story and her vision for where she is taking her business. Even though you'd only just met, you were fascinated by her company and at the end of your conversation you found yourself buzzing with potential, inspired and eager to get back to the office and begin emulating her success in your own business!

Early on in my career as an IT business owner, I was very fortunate to spend time with some of the most inspirational and successful people in the IT industry. Just being around these people inspired me and encouraged me to emulate them and raise my game to a new level. What's more, I quickly found that these type of people were more than happy to answer my questions on how they achieved their success – each of them giving generously of their time and experience to help me grow as an IT business owner.

Many of the ideas and strategies I share with you in this very book were taught to me by the positive, successful people I surrounded myself with then – and still seek out to spend time with to this day.

I'd encourage you to pay attention to the type of people you are currently spending time with.

- Are they generally positive or negative with their words and actions?
- Do they speak well of and introduce you to others you can learn from, or do they gossip and speak ill of others?
- Are they ambitious and growing their businesses, or are they in the same spot now that they were three years ago?
- Do you come away from meetings with them inspired and full of energy, or lethargic and listless?

Just by spending time with people who are positive and successful, you'll find that you become more positive and successful yourself. But be aware, spend time with negative people, and you should expect negative results.

So where can you find these positive, successful people to surround yourself with?

Attend user groups or peer groups

It can be a lonely life being an IT business owner. Even if you have employees or a business partner, chances are that the majority of problems and big decisions within your business fall upon you and you alone.

But the fact is, you're not the only one who feels this way. Any problem you're experiencing, someone else has experienced before. Any challenge you're facing, someone just like you has faced before.

Who are these people who have faced the same problems as you?

Dealt with the same challenges?

They are your peers, and in some cases, your competitors.

"Hold on a minute, Richard!" I hear you say. "You're suggesting I talk to my competitors about my business?"

Absolutely. Not only talk to them, but befriend them and share your knowledge and experience with them.

"But, but!" I hear you go on, exasperated. "They'll steal my clients!"

Well, they might, but in my experience there are enough clients for everyone – regardless of what geography you are in – and you stand to gain a lot more from talking to your peers than you'll lose from NOT talking to them!

My own IT business was built off the back of peer relationships. As well as attending local user groups, where I learned about the latest products and solutions from vendors, the latest trends in the industry, valuable technical advice and guidance I could take back to my business, I also joined advanced peer groups – or "mastermind" groups – where I and other IT businesses, including, in some cases, my direct competitors, openly shared their challenges, their victories and their failures, all in the spirit of learning from each other and growing their own business.

You may still be sceptical, and I understand that, but think back to our earlier look at surrounding yourself with positive, successful people. I'm willing to bet that in every example of an interaction you've had with someone who is positive and successful – someone who inspired you to approach them for advice and guidance – that person gave freely of their time and experience to help you.

Were they worried about giving away "trade secrets"? Were they concerned that you'd take what they told you and use it to compete with them?

No, they weren't concerned, because they understood that none of what they had learned is a trade secret. Anything they could tell you, you could easily go and find on the Internet – if you looked hard enough. But by taking an interest in and helping others, they realised that others took an interest and helped them. In short, everyone grows through mutual gain, and that's the philosophy that IT user groups and peer groups are built on.

Such groups vary in size and makeup, but generally speaking, you can find a user group near to you wherever you are in the world. These user groups typically meet regularly in a relaxed, informal environment, and often feature a speaker who will share education, while the rest of the group chip in with ideas, challenges, news and feedback that benefits everyone in the room.

Other groups, such as the Heartlands Technology Group (HTG) and the IT trade association CompTIA, have more formal arrangements with membership requirements and quarterly meetings where deep levels of trust are built up and maintained between members. Joining such groups will exponentially increase your learning – provided you are committed to also being a giver and not just a taker in such communities.

And if you can't find a local user group or peer group, why not start a group yourself and invite other local IT businesses to join you?

Even if it's a regular get together over coffee with another local IT business who you are friendly with, you'll find that such meetings can help you overcome challenges, whether they be technical or business in nature. These meetings can inspire and motivate you to keep pushing forwards – to get better at what you do.

In conclusion, the most successful IT business owners I've ever experienced had one thing in common – all of them spent time with other successful IT business owners in a peer or user group. Make sure you do too.

Further Reading

- HTG Peer Groups – https://www.htgpeergroups.com/
- Taylor Business Improvement Groups – https://www.taylorbusinessgroup.com/businessimprovementgroups
- CompTIA – http://www.comptia.org
- A list of user groups for UK Managed Service Providers http://tubb.co/1MeOnif
- 3 good reasons to attend your local user group meeting http://tubb.co/1Srj4j4

Attend conferences and seminars

Every month, wherever you are in the world, IT business owners are spoiled with options when it comes to conferences and seminars that can help them learn about industry trends, discover best practices and grow their IT business.

Whether it is trade associations putting on annual conferences, large vendors staging community events, distributors and suppliers putting together expos, or other vendors putting together local seminar and "lunch and learn" events – the biggest challenge IT business owners should face is in choosing which events NOT to go to, not which events they should!

Why then do so many IT business owners never attend any conferences? Why do they not take time out of the office to learn about new products or strategies that can help their businesses?

The key reason I hear for not taking advantage of these opportunities is... time.

"I don't have time to be out of the office," some IT business owners will tell me, or "I'm just too busy to go to these events," others will say.

I understand fully. The life of an IT business owner is one that is hectic and busy, with demands on your time every minute of every day.

But if you're constantly reacting to the work in front of you, how do you ever find the time to grow and achieve your goals for the business?

My mentor, MSP business owner Gareth Brown, shared with me that he looks at his day as a timeline. Everything takes up some space on that timeline. The timeline is fragmented with tasks, calls, checks and other jobs. Gareth suggests that you imagine running a defrag on this timeline which results in you batching tasks together to do everything more efficiently.

In my opinion, and based on my experiences of working with the most successful IT business owners in the world, taking time out of the office to attend IT conferences and seminars is not a "nice to have" option, it is a "must do" option.

Attending such events enables you to gain a valuable perspective into the emerging trends of the IT industry. It enables you to hear, often for little or no cost (beyond your own time and travel expenses) the opinions and advice of some of the best people in our industry. Attending such events gives you an insight into what others are doing to grow their IT businesses, and a perspective to how you might do better with your own IT business.

This perspective is something often overlooked. Being in the office all day, every day, working, working, working on your business is admirable. But by doing so, you lose perspective. By being so close to your work, you start to overlook what others on the outside can see. Attending events gives you valuable time away from the office – time to pause and consider whether what you are doing is the right strategy, and if not, how it can be changed.

Unsure which events are for you? Well, such events aren't hard to find. Ask any vendor if they have events coming up and they'll typically give you a long list. Trade associations such as CompTIA have gatherings across the globe throughout the year. And I've included links to events calendars worldwide in my "Further Reading" section at the end of this chapter. Make sure you get out there, visit these events and reap the rewards!

Be present during presentations

The speakers at such events, whether it be a large IT conference or a small local seminar, are usually some of the most successful and experienced people in the IT industry and they often offer up invaluable information to their audiences – for free!

Yet despite the value that is offered from such speakers, I'm still flabbergasted to look around any audience and see that there are people not paying attention. IT business owners who are trying to multi-task – listening to a highly paid speaker delivering nuggets of wisdom, while also trying to remote control a server issue, or read and reply to email, or worse (and fairly unforgivably, in my opinion) catch up on Facebook.

Don't be that person. We already know that multitasking is impossible, that we're merely dividing our focus between two things and doing neither well. When you're in a presentation, be present – pay attention to what the speaker is saying. Learn from them. Make notes, if you need to, but do so with a pen and paper. Turn your smartphone and tablet off and devote your attention to absorbing the valuable information the speaker has to offer.

Any emails you have, any issues that have arisen, any crises that have emerged (and they typically never do, despite our worse fears) can wait an hour or so for us to deal with. And if you believe they can't, then I'd ask you to re-evaluate your own sense of importance and work on adjusting that instead.

If there is a highly paid, successful speaker delivering his wisdom to an audience, then do yourself a favour and pay attention. Be present. You'll be glad you did.

Further Reading

- A list of IT channel events for MSPs in the UK and Europe – http://www.tubblog.co.uk/?s=Channel+Events

Go networking

I can't tell you the amount of times I've attended IT conferences as an IT business owner and found myself coming back to the office with renewed energy, enthusiasm and ideas that propelled my business forwards. Yet each time I attended such a conference, I always had pangs of guilt that I should be in the office doing more work. If you have ever felt this way too, then remind yourself that attending such events isn't a "jolly" – it's valuable business owners' thinking and learning time.

That said, such events are rarely anything less than a lot of fun, as well as educational. While the event presentations are often very valuable, the real value in any of these events is that it typically brings together some of the best people in our industry under one roof. The value to be found in networking with your most successful peers and suppliers is immense. The conversations you have over impromptu cups of coffee, chats in the corridors and hallways, and yes, in-depth conversations in the bars and restaurants – these are all nuggets that any successful IT business owner will tell you have helped propel their business forwards.

If you have the opportunity to review the attendee list of any seminar or conference ahead of time, do so. You can highlight any people you'd like to spend time with and seek them out to suggest you meet up at the event. If you're unsure who is attending, why not ask on social media? It's a good way to make sure people know you are attending such events and seek you out.

Whatever you do, though, do get out there and meet people. You'll learn so much from others and come away with ideas, energy and enthusiasm that you can't get anywhere else.

Keeping up to date online

With all the trade publications, blog posts, magazines, videos and audio podcasts out there, how can you possibly be expected to stay up to date?

The key is not to try to consume everything, but to look for opportunities to filter the information so you're just seeing the things that are important to you.

In an earlier chapter we talked about the need to reduce the amount of emails we receive and process. The same is true for other information sources.

I use tools such as Feedly (https://feedly.com) to subscribe to RSS feeds, meaning my favourite blog posts are always up to date for me to read at my leisure or when I need a shot of inspiration or motivation.

Another way to filter the information you receive is to continuously reassess your magazine subscriptions. Do you genuinely read all those magazines you subscribe to, or do you do so out of fear of missing out on something? If you've managed to get by without reading those magazines, cancel the subscriptions. It will be one less thing to distract you or make you feel bad about not dealing with.

Where possible, move away from printed magazines to digital equivalents. The Google Newsstand and other digital magazine equivalents gives me the opportunity to read the magazines of my choice rather than whatever I can find when I'm on a long train or plane journey.

Talking of travelling, it's an ideal time for you to listen to podcasts. I listen to short podcasts of 3-5 minutes while I'm killing time queueing or in a waiting room. I listen to podcasts of 15-25 minutes while walking between locations. I also listen to long-form podcasts of an hour plus when I'm driving longer distances. Podcasts are a great way to keep up to date on industry trends and to be inspired by the most successful, positive people in our space.

Then there is YouTube. The world's top video site has more content than you could ever consume. Don't be distracted by going down the rabbit hole of trying to watch interesting videos as you find them. Instead, add videos to your "Watch Later" list and then consume when it's convenient to you. My "Watch Later" list is always being updated with TED talks or other inspiring videos that I can conveniently watch during my breakfast each morning. I find this is an inspiring way for me to start my day!

Realise that you don't need to be a victim of information overload. Use technology and techniques that can help you stay connected and up to date – on your terms.

Further Reading

- Feedly – https://feedly.com/
- Google Newsstand – https://play.google.com/store/newsstand?hl=en_GB
- A list of channel trade publications for UK IT companies http://tubb.co/1OjEy0H
- Why you should listen to podcasts for personal development http://tubb.co/1RBXu0c
- TubbTalk – The Podcast for IT Consultants – http://tubb.co/TubbTalk
- Tubblog YouTube channel – http://tubb.co/TubbTube
- TED talks for small business owners http://tubb.co/1gF5s83

Coaches and mentors

Right at the start of this chapter I suggested that every IT business owner should spend time around positive, successful people.

Joining user groups and peer groups gives you access to such people. Regularly attending IT conferences and seminars puts you in the same space as the best in our industry too. But if you really want to benefit from the wisdom and advice of those who have been there and done it, I'd recommend you look into working with a coach or mentor.

Both coaches and mentors are typically individuals with high levels of experience in the IT industry – either as a technician or business owner, and often both. They are people who have committed their lives to self-development and learning, soaking up knowledge from their own mentors and coaches, and now find themselves in a position where others can learn from them too. Working with a coach or mentor gives you access to wisdom and experience that can help propel your personal development and your business growth.

What is a mentor?

Firstly, it's worth defining the difference between a coach and a mentor. Many people interchange the two terms, but in my experience, a mentor is somebody who gives freely of their time and experience to help you. For instance, in our industry, a mentor may be somebody who is retired, or even someone who still runs an IT business but agrees to share some of his time and experience with you to help your own development. Why would they do this? Well, for the most part, most mentors are grateful for those wonderful individuals who gave of their time and experience to help **them** earlier in their career and honour their own mentors by "paying it forwards". Others just enjoy helping others.

If you're able to find a mentor, then I'd encourage you to do so. It's my experience that mentors often appear in your life rather than you seeking them out. They are the people you meet at conferences and seminars who you strike up conversations with and find inspirational. You build a relationship with them over time. Sometimes mentorships are formal – where you ask the person to mentor you and you get together at agreed dates and times. Other times mentorships are informal – the person is on the other end of a telephone or email to help you as and when.

I've been fortunate enough to have a number of amazing mentors in my life. For instance, my good friend and mentor John Shufflebottom is a semi-retired professional who has spent most of his life at the board level in large IT businesses and not-for-profit organisations. John enjoys helping others and long after we'd first met, and indeed moved away from working with each other at a mutual client of ours, John and I stayed in touch, with John kindly offering his advice and guidance to me whenever I have needed it.

Another valued mentor of mine, my close friend Gareth Brown, still runs an IT business, Sytec, based in Salisbury within the UK. I first met Gareth at a Microsoft event where, as a fledgling IT business owner myself, I watched in awe as he spoke about what it took to grow an IT business. Immediately after he finished speaking I approached Gareth for advice, and I'm very grateful to say, years later he still offers me advice and wisdom by telephone as needed or over a cup of tea whenever we have the opportunity to get together in person.

What is a coach?

As a mentor is giving freely of their time and experience, of course you must be respectful of putting too many demands on them. They have their own lives to be getting on with.

Which is why, in addition to having mentors, I've always made sure to work with one or more coaches to help me grow at a rate I am comfortable with.

A coach is someone you pay to offer you specific learning or guidance. For instance, over the years I have surrounded myself with a number of coaches who have helped me with everything from learning to be a better public speaker to marketing my services online.

For the past few years I've worked with a business coach, my good friend Alan Matthews, who meets me in person every month to discuss anything and everything related to my business growth. He encourages me on, helps keep me grounded with an impartial perspective, and holds me accountable for executing my ideas. Alan works with a number of business owners in this way, and I find my investment in his monthly retainer to be invaluable.

The accountability aspect of working with a coach cannot be underestimated. If you're somebody like me who has a lot of great ideas but struggles to finish them then a coach can help keep you on task and, if you stray from the path towards completion, help you understand why this is and help you get back on course. One of my great mentors, Arlin Sorensen, regularly used to say: "Vision without execution is hallucination". A coach helps you to avoid hallucinating, and get busy executing ideas.

Whether it be a coach who you pay to work with you regularly on one or more specific areas, and/or a mentor who gives their time and experience freely to you, the benefits of seeking out someone to provide you with guidance and accountability cannot be underestimated. You will find you grow as an individual, as a leader and, subsequently, your business will grow too.

In short, by working with a coach or mentor you're learning from somebody who knows what they are talking about and can teach you to do better. Anyone who has experienced any degree of success – and even those who have reached the pinnacle of their profession and want to keep on learning – works with a coach and/or a mentor. I'd encourage you to do so too.

Further Reading

- MSP business wingman – http://www.mspwingman.co.uk
- Transmentum – http://www.transmentum.co.uk/
- 5 Things to look for when choosing an executive coach – http://tubb.co/1SrjeXO

Chapter 9: What to do when you know you should stay in touch with clients more but you don't have the time

One of the challenges of being a busy IT business owner is staying in touch with your clients. Sure, they'll contact you when something goes wrong with their IT – but do you really want the only time you ever speak to your clients to be when they are asking you for help?

Most progressive IT business owners realise they need to stay in touch with their clients regularly to maintain the relationship. Regular contact with your clients can help you build bonding and rapport, which leads to your client being loyal to your business and can mean you retain their custom when your competitors come sniffing around.

Maintaining regular contact with your clients can also uncover issues – often minor issues that fester if left unaddressed – before they become major complaints that can develop into major issues that you are then scrambling to address.

It's also worth remembering that maintaining regular contact with your clients can uncover all manner of opportunities. I can't tell you the number of times I've telephoned a client to see how they are, only for the client to tell me: "I'm glad you've called, it's reminded me we need a new PC/server/entire IT Infrastructure!"

Staying in regular contact with your clients – and not just waiting for them to contact you when they need your help – is a powerful way to retain your clients' business and increase the business they do with you.

So you know you should stay in touch with your clients more than you currently do, but what if you don't have the time? In this chapter we'll explore some techniques for staying in touch with your clients that won't take you much time or energy, but will reap big rewards.

Using "just in time" social media

Does your IT business use social media to stay in touch with clients? Most IT businesses think of social media as a marketing method – a way of finding new clients and winning their business – but they overlook how social media can be used to build upon relationships with existing clients.

There is a wealth of information to be found within the updates your clients post to their social media feeds – but as busy IT business owners, you can often overlook this information and fail to use it when you need it most.

It's easy to see why. Social media channels such as Twitter and LinkedIn can sometimes feel like a torrent of information that threatens to drown you. How can you dig out the information relevant to your clients amongst all the noise?

If you're a Microsoft Outlook user, then I'd encourage you to check out the Outlook Social Connector add-in. It's a free download from Microsoft, and once installed will pull in information from your clients' (and any other contacts') social media feeds and display them to you whenever you open an email or address book entry for that person.

The application here is simple. The next time you go to email, telephone or meet with your client, open up Outlook and check out their latest social media updates. Your client might be posting details of a job vacancy – in which case you can drop into your conversation with them that they may need additional hardware or licenses to support that new hire when they start – avoiding that all-too-common scenario where the client telephones you on a Monday morning to say, "We've got a new person starting, can you set up a PC for them please? When? Well, today!"

Similarly, your client may have just posted a status update expressing pride in their child having won at school sports day. When you speak to your client, merely mentioning "I noticed your son/daughter won a prize, you must be very proud!" is sure to set the conversation off on the right foot.

If you're a Google Apps user, then a similar application is a Google Chrome plug-in called Rapportive. Once installed, Rapportive draws information about contacts from LinkedIn, Twitter, Facebook and other social media platforms to give you an "at a glance" view of their latest activity – providing you with the information you need to build rapport with your client.

Never underestimate the power of showing a client that they are important to you by taking an interest in and asking them about the things that are important to them. They're making this information available for you to use – make sure you use it to maintain your client relationships.

Further Reading

- Introduction to the Outlook Social Connector – https://support.office.com/en-NZ/article/Introduction-to-the-Outlook-Social-Connector-54bf57cf-0b9c-4230-9776-1f028550bb07
- Rapportive for Google Mail – https://rapportive.com/
- FullContact – https://www.fullcontact.com/

Saying "thank you" to clients

When was the last time you thanked one of your clients for their business? If your answer is "Well, I'm sure they know how grateful I am!" then you're missing a trick. If your answer is "They should be thankful to us for all we do for them!" then stop for a minute and think if they would see your relationship in the same way!

Showing appreciation to your clients is important. It's important to let them know you value your relationship with them. It's important to maintain your relationship and prevent your competitors from stealing business away from you. Most importantly, showing gratitude is the right thing to do and will make the work you do much more fun!

Some of us feel uncomfortable showing gratitude. They wonder how a client will react. Let me say that in all the years of running an IT business, I've never once had a client react badly when I told them, "I'm grateful for you trusting us with your business." Quite the opposite. Clients are humbled when you share your gratitude, and often reciprocate, sharing with you how valuable they find your way. There is power in saying "thank you" out loud.

Send a thank you note

One example of showing gratitude that is low effort but high impact is the simple act of sending a thank you note. Whenever a client renewed their contract with us, I sent them a handwritten thank you note expressing gratitude for their trust in us. Whenever a client spoke well of us to someone – perhaps a referral or an introduction – I sent them a thank you note.

Writing a note of gratitude takes mere minutes – but can have a high impact. Most people like the idea of writing a thank you note but never get around to it because they turn it into a chore. They need to make time to buy the card, stamp the envelope, etc. This is easily solved. Set yourself a reminder to go to the local card store and buy a dozen different "Thank You!" cards and keep them in stock. While you're there, pop into the Post Office and buy a dozen stamps. The next time you think you might want to send a thank you note, grab a card from stock, write it and post it. Simple.

You might be surprised to know that even when clients complain we show gratitude through handwritten notes. "What!" I hear you say. "You thanked a client for complaining?!" On one particular occasion my own IT business screwed up the billing for a client. We sent the client an invoice with the wrong amount, at the wrong time of the month. Not surprisingly, we received a very irate telephone call from a lady who worked for the client. I say not surprisingly, because the lady – who was the client's finance manager and paid all their suppliers – was in the middle of her month end routine and was rather stressed with her workload. We didn't help her by sending her the wrong invoice and she told us as much. We naturally apologised and offered to deal with the situation, which she seemed satisfied with, but I took the opportunity to send this lady a thank you card and a box of chocolates. The thank you card expressed our gratitude for the fact that as finance manager, she had always ensured we were paid on time – which we very much appreciated. The chocolates were to say sorry for adding to her workload unnecessarily when we knew how hard she worked and how we'd added to that workload. Upon receiving the card and chocolates, the lady telephoned us and told us how we had made her month – she had a beaming smile and really appreciated our gesture and she told us how she'd continue to make sure we were paid on time each month.

In this case, our mistake may have caused ill-feeling with the client – but the simple act of showing gratitude turned the situation from a negative scenario into a positive one.

In a world of instant messages, email, social media and text messages it's so rare nowadays to receive a handwritten note. Make sure you stand out from the crowd by sending such notes to your clients.

Take your clients a box of donuts

The next time you are visiting your client – be it a support visit, or just popping by to see how they are – first pop by your local bakery or Dunkin' Donuts outlet, buy a box of their freshest, finest donuts, and take them with you to your client site.

I have never – and I do mean never – had a client complain that you've brought some delicious-smelling, sweet-tasting donuts for them to eat! Sure, they may grumble that you aren't helping their waistline – but they surely won't pass up the opportunity to enjoy a treat!

I know of some of clients in my coaching business – IT Solution Providers and Managed Service Providers – who have accounts with local cupcake specialists who will deliver tasty treats to their clients on their behalf! What a wonderful idea! Even if you can't make the time to visit a client, why not send them some confectionery to express your gratitude for their business.

Small gestures like a simple box of donuts or a basket of cupcakes can make the difference between your client viewing you as just another supplier, or as a business partner they know, like and trust.

Further Reading

- Why it always pays to say thank you – http://tubb.co/1Srju9d
- We must find time to stop and thank the people who make a difference in our lives http://tubb.co/1MeSx9T

Asking your client how you are doing

How often do you ask your clients "Are you happy with our service?" If you answered "Not very often" then you're not alone. Most IT businesses do a frankly woeful job of making sure their clients are happy with the service and only find out when something is wrong when it's too late – when the client tells you they're deeply unhappy, or worse, that they are moving their business to a new IT partner.

Set yourself a reminder on your calendar to make one phone call a week to a client to simply ask them, "How are we doing?" Many businesses think that sending an email or survey to ask this question will have the same impact. It won't. Taking a few minutes out of your day once a week to ask them personally will, however, send a message that your client is important to you.

The simple act of picking up the phone and asking the question will have powerful results. The client may say: "You're doing great, but I appreciate you asking!" or they may say, "Actually, there is something I'd like to talk to you about" – giving you the opportunity to address an issue that may have festered unless it was brought to the surface.

Some clients are grudging with their praise. They may answer your question with an "Ok I guess, but it'd be nice if we saw you more often" or similar feedback. You can immediately take steps to make sure you visit the client more often to see how they are.

However your client answers, they are giving you valuable feedback that you can use to improve your service and retain the clients business. So set that recurring reminder in your calendar and take five minutes a week to ensure you make a call to your client – it may be the best five minutes you spend each week.

Doing client floor walks

One of the tenets of managed services is scalability. With a service desk of three engineers, you might serve 100 or more clients with thousands of workstations and hundreds of servers. Remote monitoring and management tools can alert your business to issues on your client site before they even know about them. Remote desktop access tools allow you to connect to your client sites and quickly resolve issues without ever leaving your desk.

The trouble is, if you maintain your client sites remotely and if your client never sees an engineer on site, they assume you don't love them – or worse, aren't spending time looking after them. Yes, it's illogical – but your clients are human beings, and we base decisions on emotions, not logic.

I'm not suggesting for a moment that you start dispatching engineers to drive across town to deal with missing files that can be restored remotely, or crawl through traffic to update a client's web browser instead of deploying that software from the comfort of your own desk – but showing face at a client site is a powerful way to show your client you love them and uncover issues you may not have been aware of.

When I ran my own IT business, I often dispatched engineers to visit a client to do what we called a "floor walk". The engineer would visit the site under the pretext of doing some maintenance – but upon arrival would let the office manager or receptionist know that they would be happy to help with any issues while they were there.

Quite often the engineer would uncover all manner of niggling issues. A printer not functioning. A mouse that behaved erratically. A monitor that was out of focus. Why didn't users report these issues so they could be dealt with? The most common answer: "We didn't want to bother you with something so trivial."

I once received a complaint from a client about a PC that had been behaving erratically and repeatedly crashing over a six month period. "I'm so sorry to hear that. When did you first report it to us?" I asked, expecting to have to go on to apologise for our lack of resolution. "Oh, we've never reported it – but surely you should just know about it!" the client responded. I could see their point – we often extolled the virtues of our remote monitoring and maintenance solution – so why didn't we know about it? A floor walk of the client site may have revealed this issue, offering us the opportunity to resolve the issue and avoid a client complaint.

Floor walks often uncover sales opportunities too. I gave a bonus to my engineers whenever they uncovered a sales opportunity – and this encouraged them to go floor walking more often. An engineer once came back to me with an opportunity to provide a client with a whole new telephone system after he performed a floor walk at a client site and heard numerous grumbles about the client losing telephone calls because of their existing aging telephone system. Other engineer floor walks regularly uncovered replacement PC orders, new printers and workstation upgrades – all because they'd walked the client's office and asked people if they could help with anything, and uncovered issues that were costing the client through lost time and productivity.

So schedule floor walks into your diary. Encourage engineers to visit client sites – as and when they have the time available – and do a floor walk to look for issues. At worst they'll uncover some niggling problems and nip them in the bud – but don't be surprised if they also uncover sales opportunities!

Further Reading

- How to avoid your client asking you: "What are we paying you for?" http://tubb.co/1MeSZ82

Chapter 10: How to have more energy when you're too busy to stay healthy

When you're busy and there are a lot of demands on your time there's a tendency to believe that if you just put in the extra effort, working longer and harder today, then you will overcome the "hump" and tomorrow things will be calmer.

You've probably been there yourself (or may still be there). Just this once you start early and finish late. Just this once you skip sleep in favour of catching up on work. Just this once you skip lunch in favour of getting ahead on a project. Just this once you eat whatever is to hand while at your desk.

The trouble is, all of these short-cuts aren't taken "just this once". They typically happen again and again, and before you know it, it's the new normal.

It's surprising how long it can take us to realise that this state of being a busy IT business owner – one with too many demands on their time – isn't something that will go away anytime soon. In fact, as your business becomes more successful the demands on your time will increase! You'll feel as though you have to go with even less sleep. You'll have even less time to eat. You'll feel as though you need to spend even more time at work.

Continuing to burn the candle at both ends is not a sustainable technique for growing an IT business. Regardless of all the macho nonsense that comes with phrases such as "sleep/lunch/holidays are for wimps", there's one phrase I was taught years ago that is much more accurate: "Being dead is bad for business."

Being dead is bad for business

A mentor of mine shared this phrase with me when I was complaining to him once about the long hours I put in at the office. I was bemoaning the fact I was consistently working evenings and weekends and that I hadn't experienced a holiday in some time. I shared how my blood pressure was up, causing me to feel tired, sluggish and irritable all the time, and how I'd piled weight on, thanks to spending all hours in the office and eating whatever was on hand while I was "on the hoof".

Of course, I was a young man when my mentor first shared the phrase "Being dead is bad for business" with me, and the idea of me actually keeling over because of the strain I was putting on my body by building my business felt rather far-fetched (although it certainly doesn't now I'm older and wiser). But it did make me realise that I was going about my mountain of responsibilities and ever-growing To-Do list in entirely the wrong way.

Throwing yourself into work in the hope you'll get ahead isn't the solution, because as soon as you've got this lot of responsibilities dealt with, another equal or greater amount will fill your plate. I'm not saying that hard work isn't required in growing a successful IT business – it most certainly is – but holding the belief that consistently working long hours and weekends, and looking upon eating and sleeping as an inconvenient interruption to your work day, is nothing short of crazy.

If you want to get more done at work, then first and foremost look after yourself – physically and mentally.

If you realise that this new state of business with ever increasing demands and interruptions isn't exceptional – it's the new norm – then you can also realise that you need to find long-term coping techniques that allow you to not only survive, but thrive, long term.

You need to look after yourself and have the energy to consistently do what you need to do.

Before you throw your hands in the air and tell me that you genuinely are too busy to stay healthy, let me say that this idea isn't all "new age" thinking or "in an ideal world" rhetoric. It's a simple reality. If you look after yourself, you'll have more energy to do the important things you need to do to grow your IT business. If you don't, you'll run yourself into the ground and lose health, wealth and relationships along the way. I've seen it happen.

Looking after yourself doesn't mean becoming an ultra-fit marathon runner, nor does it mean spending every hour in the gym. Instead, here are some simple, easy to implement practices that you can build into useful habits in your routine.

Sleep is NOT for wimps

You're probably familiar with the expression "sleep is for wimps" – often bandied about by those individuals who want to project an image of a high-achieving go-getter, working hard to get ahead when others are sleeping.

The trouble is, we all need sleep – it's part and parcel of being human. You may as well say "breathing is for wimps!" as "sleep is for wimps" – it's equally as ludicrous to think you can go without either.

I'm not suggesting for a minute that there aren't times when you will need to pull a late one at the office, but when it becomes a regular habit – that isn't sustainable.

Many of us regularly walk around like zombies – perpetually sleep deprived. Typically, we need 7-8 hours' sleep per night and if we don't get it, our performance becomes impaired. We might think we're achieving more by cutting back on sleep, but in reality, we're getting less achieved by going without sleep.

Sadly, few of us nowadays have good bedtime habits. For the typical IT business owner, try these simple tactics to make sure you get the right amount of good quality sleep every night.

- **Set an alarm**. Try to maintain the same sleep routine, going to bed at the same time and waking up at the same time every day. Your body will become accustomed to this routine and help you sleep accordingly. If a loud buzzer isn't your ideal way of being woken each day (and it certainly isn't mine!) then you might consider using a natural light alarm clock to gently wake you each day rather than an audible alarm that wrenches you out of a deep sleep. Lastly, if you struggle to maintain a bedtime routine, consider setting an alarm to remind you to go to bed!
- **No screens before bedtime.** Taking your smartphone or tablet to bed is a sure-fire way of keeping you awake. Bombarding yourself with the latest social media updates from a glowing smartphone screen and opening yourself up to text and instant messages from your night-owl friends contributes towards keeping your mind active – not relaxed. Instead, set yourself a rule of "no screens before bedtime". If you need to read something in bed to take your mind off the day and relax, take a good old-fashioned paperback book instead.
- **Don't keep your phone next to your bed.** Once your phone is turned off, put it away in a separate room to charge overnight. Even a phone that is turned off and within our eye line can be a distraction and will set your mind thinking of tasks related to your phone – work, email, social media. Move the phone to another room and forget about it until you awake refreshed the next day.

- **Avoid reading emails when you wake up.** For many of us, looking at our phone before we've even got out of bed in the morning is routine. The trouble is, even glancing at a new email we've received overnight will set our mind running away with thoughts of the contents of **that** email – distracting us from focusing on what we really should be doing. Even glancing at the subject lines of new emails in your inbox is enough to distract us. Instead, resist the urge to read emails until you've accomplished one important thing for that day. Doing so will help you remain focused and achieving the important tasks.

Sleep is an important element to ensuring we are at our best, have our wits about us, focused on getting important work done, and have the willpower to get that work done.

Lack of sleep means we can be lethargic, easily distracted and have low willpower – making us prone to all manner of bad habits.

Make sure you put sleep high on your list of priorities – and not as an afterthought.

Further Reading

- This is what happens when you don't get enough sleep – http://www.mindbodygreen.com/0-13486/this-is-what-happens-when-you-dont-get-enough-sleep-infographic.html
- Royal College of Psychiatrists' leaflet on sleeping well – http://www.rcpsych.ac.uk/healthadvice/problemsdisorders/sleepingwell.aspx
- Why not enough sleep will make your life a nightmare – http://www.express.co.uk/life-style/health/422881/Why-not-enough-sleep-will-make-your-life-a-nightmare

- Sleep deprivation damaging businesses – http://www.hrmagazine.co.uk/hr/news/1150030/sleep-deprivation-damaging-business
- 5 reasons you shouldn't use your iPhone in bed – http://www.gottabemobile.com/2015/02/23/iphone-in-bed/
- Should I keep my smartphone and tablet out of the bedroom? – http://www.theguardian.com/lifeandstyle/2013/jun/09/smartphones-tablets-in-bedroom-sleep
- Why you shouldn't read a tablet before bed – http://time.com/3642620/why-you-shouldnt-read-a-tablet-before-bed/
- Chronic lack of sleep affects one in three British workers – http://www.theguardian.com/lifeandstyle/2012/apr/01/chronic-sleep-deprivation-uk-staff
- Reading on a screen before bed might be killing you – http://www.huffingtonpost.com/2014/12/23/reading-before-bed_n_6372828.html

Take breaks regularly

As an IT business owner, you've got a lot to do each day. Let's be honest, it probably feels like too much to do each day.

When faced with an ever increasing To-Do list and a mountain of demands, the logical solution seems to be to work harder. By working longer, and harder, you'll get more done. Right?

Except as human beings we're not designed to work that way. We need rest and recuperation to function at our best – otherwise we're simply putting in the hours under the illusion of being busy.

You're probably familiar with the type of people who live under the illusion of being busy. They typically work at their desks through their lunch and work late in the office each night, getting stuff done. They are forever busy and seem chained to their desk for long periods at a time. I may have just struck a nerve and you might recognise yourself in this category.

In my experience, those people who work in this way actually get the least amount achieved – or if they do get more work done, it's not to a high quality. "Being on" for long periods of time in this way is not conducive to high quality work and at best is a sort of martyrdom.

By regularly taking breaks throughout your day, you can get more achieved. Even a five minute break to get up and stretch your legs, grab a glass of water and take your mind off work is enough to re-energise you to get more done when you sit back at your desk again. Incorporate lots of five minute breaks into your day and see the difference.

Don't skip lunch breaks. Get away from your desk – and preferably the office – and take your mind off work. You'll come back with more energy and enthusiasm to get the important work done.

Take holidays. As an IT business owner it can be hard to schedule the traditional week away, so why not schedule lots of long weekends where you can relax, turn off your smartphone, leave your emails behind and recuperate.

Taking a break is not a sign of weakness. Working longer and harder will not necessarily give you an advantage. Incorporating regular breaks into your days, weeks and years will help you produce to a higher level – and enable you to work smarter.

Further Reading

- Scheduling a 15 minute break can help productivity – http://www.reresourcegroup.co.uk/scheduling-15-minute-break-can-help-productivity/

Why successful business owners read books

For the most successful IT business owners I've observed, reading regularly seems to be a key to success.

Building a habit of regularly reading – whether it be business strategy advice, self-development books, biographies of the rich and famous or even a good old-fashioned fiction paperback – can help you find focus, fresh ideas and enthusiasm for improving your business and yourself.

How is this possible? "Surely reading a sci-fi fiction book won't help me improve my business?" you ask.

Have you ever worked hard thinking about how to fix a problem, but were unable to find a solution? With dogged determination you think about the issue even more – and the harder you think, the further away the problem seems to be. So you give up – for now – and go and read a book instead. While you are distracted reading the book, and quite unexpectedly, the solution to your problem pops into your head. How is this possible?

We've all experienced the situation where an idea or a solution to a problem has popped into our head at the most unexpected time. Why is this? Because when we take our mind off the problem, it gives our subconscious an opportunity to think on it – whirring away in the background until it finds a solution it can present us with. The trouble is, most of us are "on" all the time and don't give ourselves the opportunity to do subconscious thinking.

I've found that by focusing on reading regularly, I've distracted myself from day-to-day concerns and given my subconscious the opportunity to generate ideas and solutions to problems. Try it for yourself. At worst you'll take time out of your day to relax and inspire yourself with some reading, but you may just find that, regardless of the content of the book you're reading, you find yourself coming up with new ideas and solutions to problems.

Further Reading

- Why successful business leaders read regularly http://tubb.co/Y30JUX
- The books I love – http://tubb.co/1qg9m8V

Walking meetings

You know that exercise is good for you, but as an IT business owner you have an incredibly busy life. Who finds the time to go to the gym?

An excellent way to incorporate exercise into your routine is to embrace the concept of a walking meeting. Instead of sitting in a stuffy office when you're meeting with an employee, a business partner or even a client, why not get outside to walk and talk?

I regularly take walking meetings with my own clients – the owners of IT businesses – and we've found that walking and talking helps both the conversation and our ideas flow more easily. So we're getting some exercise and improving the quality of our meetings too!

Listen to podcasts

If, like most IT business owners, you are dedicated to being a high achiever and getting as much done in a day as possible, then you might struggle to make the time to do the important but not urgent things such as:

- Getting exercise
- Finding the time for strategic thinking
- Being inspired
- Keeping up to date on current industry trends

What if I told you there was a way you could achieve all of the above activities at the same time?

Every day, try plugging your headphones into your smartphone and getting out for a 30 minute walk while listening to a podcast. You'll be getting some good exercise while at the same time listening to content that will genuinely help you improve yourself and your business. Podcasts are free "on demand" radio shows, produced by some of the most inspiring hosts who share – amongst other things – some of the most insightful and motivating conversations with the world's most successful business owners.

Just 30 minutes a day taking a walk with a podcast can leave you feeling inspired, energised and full of ideas and renewed enthusiasm for your IT business and your own self-development as a leader.

I've created a list of recommended podcasts for IT business owners (http://tubb.co/RecommendedPodcasts) containing some of the world's top podcasts to help get you started, and as a bonus – why not fire up an app such as Google MyTracks (http://tubb.co/Y30mJX) which can help you track your walk each day and see your progress as you walk further and faster!

While you can easily listen to podcasts while in the car or train too (and I'd encourage you to try this as well), listening to podcasts while taking time out of my day to get some exercise has been one of the single best strategies I have used (and still use) as a business owner.

Further Reading

- DoggCatcher – the Android podcatcher – http://www.doggcatcher.com/
- Podcast app for iOS – http://support.apple.com/kb/ht3281
- 16 Windows Phone 8 podcatchers compared and reviewed http://tubb.co/1B78GpN
- Recommended podcasts for IT business owners – http://tubb.co/RecommendedPodcasts
- Google MyTracks – http://tubb.co/Y30mJX
- Why you should listen to podcasts for personal development – http://www.tubblog.co.uk/blog/2015/07/16/why-you-should-listen-to-podcasts-for-personal-development/

Building healthy habits

You'll probably have noticed that throughout this chapter I have suggested a number of activities that, when undertaken regularly, produce beneficial results for you and your business.

- Setting a "no screens before bedtime" policy
- Getting 7-8 hours of good quality sleep each night
- Not keeping your phone next to your bed
- Avoiding reading emails in the morning
- Taking regular 5 minute breaks throughout your day
- Taking a lunch break every day
- Reading books regularly
- Listening to podcasts while walking

In effect, what I'm encouraging you to do is to become aware of your existing bad habits and replace them with productive and healthy good habits.

We all have the best of intentions for doing the right thing – for ourselves, our businesses and our lifestyles. But it's easy to slip back into bad habits, so how can you ensure that you stay the course and do the things that you **know** will benefit you and not hamper your progress?

One way is to seek accountability. In an earlier chapter I mentioned that one of the benefits of working with a coach is accountability – they will ask you if you've done something you've committed to doing, and if not, why not. This helps keep you on track to do the right thing as we all like to avoid telling somebody we've not done something we promised to do.

You can also find apps to help. The app Coach.me (https://coach.me) aims to help you "succeed at everything". It helps you set and reach your goals, providing gentle reminders of your goals each day and asking you whether you've completed them. Your goals can be shared with friends and family, or the wider public, and this adds another level of accountability as others can see whether or not you've checked in and achieved what you set out to do.

Whatever steps you take to build healthier habits, look to create a level of external accountability – be it through your coaches, your friends and family or even an app or other check system like Coach.me. In holding yourself accountable to making positive changes, you're much more likely to build these changes into long-standing habits – which you will reap the rewards of every single day.

Further Reading

- Coach.me – https://www.coach.me (Feel free to search for me on Coach.me and add me as a friend too!)

- The power of habit: why we do what we do, and how to change – http://tubb.co/1Vacn9i

Chapter 11: How to quit working long hours and weekends

By this point of the book, I hope I've equipped you with some useful tactics and techniques to survive the demands placed upon you as an IT business owner. The challenge for you now is to understand that as well as being an IT business owner, you're also someone who (I'm sure) has personal commitments outside your business – a partner, family, perhaps children, as well as friends.

Even if you have none of this, you have a responsibility to yourself to live a rich and rewarding life outside of work.

It's important to remember that however hard you work at your business, there will always be more to do. Work will expand to fill the time that is available – and so you need to place parameters around when you will be working and available to be contacted, and when you will be relaxing and recharging, either alone or spending time with family and friends.

You may have already tried to do this, tried to take a break from your IT business on an evening or weekend, but found that you kept getting drawn back into work.

So how can you quit working long hours and weekends?

Disconnecting from work when at home

As the owner of your own IT business, it is important that you draw a line under the work you do in the day and define a clear "finishing" point for your work activities.

That means leaving the office (even if it's a home office) at a set time each day and resisting the temptation to do "just one more thing" before you go. As I've already mentioned, the work will expand to fill the time you make available and so while it's tempting to work late to "get on top" of things, it can quickly become a bad habit. While I'm not suggesting for a moment that you may not need to pull a late one once in a while, left unchecked, by consistently working long hours you'll inevitably become more tired and jaded, which in turn means you aren't able to perform well the following day and fall behind with work, which you then need to work late on to catch up. And so the cycle continues.

Define your working hours

Instead, have clearly defined working hours in your head. This may be 0800-1730 or 0900-1700 – you choose. Do what you are able to achieve during the day, and then, when it comes to your finishing time, take 5 minutes to brainstorm anything that is left unfinished. Resist the urge to "just get it done" there and then, and write down the actions that you need to take the following day. By doing so, you'll be able to get the work out of your head and relax with an understanding of what you'll be working on when you return to the office.

Once you've defined a clear "finishing point" and clarified what you'll be working on the next day, resist the urge to revisit work for the remainder of the evening. That means disconnecting from work when you are at home and resisting swapping working on your laptop in the office for working on your smartphone from your sofa at home.

Use separate work and personal profiles

With many of us having a single smartphone, tablet or laptop for both work and personal pursuits, it can blur the line unhealthily between work and pleasure. You're distracted by emails while you're supposed to be relaxing and, vice versa, you're distracted by Facebook when you're supposed to be working! Consider setting up separate work and personal profiles on your devices to minimise these distractions and allow you to use the same device for work when in the office and pleasure when at home.

If you're of a nature that is unable to resist temptation – perhaps thinking you can "just take a peek" at work emails during your downtime – you may wish to disconnect completely when you get home of an evening. Turn your smartphone off and put it in a drawer until the next day. I can assure you the world will continue turning and your business will still be there in the morning.

Further Reading

- What is it like to disconnect from the Internet for a day? http://tubb.co/1OjLUS5

Set expectations on your availability

While ignoring the temptation to work when at home is difficult at the best of times, when work rudely forces itself into your home life it can become even more challenging.

Emails and telephone calls can interrupt your home life – if you let them.

Ensure you set clear expectations with staff, suppliers and clients on your availability of an evening and a weekend. Share with them via email and written letter the hours you work and what they should expect if they try to contact you out of hours or during a weekend.

Even then, you can expect some clients to think the rules don't apply to them and they can call you when they choose. Here are some tips for dealing with those clients.

Use voicemail to screen calls

In my early days as an MSP owner, I never answered clients' calls on an evening or a weekend. I always let clients leave a voicemail, which I vetted before deciding to return their call. If their server was on fire, then that was an emergency that I might respond to after a given period of time – say, 30 minutes.

Why 30 minutes? An immediate response conditions the client into believing that you are there, ready and waiting for any call they may make. Instead, try calling back after 30 minutes and start the conversation by saying, "Sorry I missed your call, I was having dinner with my family/visiting the cinema/at a dinner party with friends" – anything that highlights that you have a life that your client is interrupting by calling out of hours.

If you screen their voicemail and they are working late and simply trying to figure out an Excel spreadsheet and want to pick your brains, then that can wait until the morning – however urgent they may think it is. Return the call the next day by saying: "Sorry I missed your call, I was having dinner with my family/visiting the cinema/at a dinner party with friends and didn't turn my phone on until I'd got home and by then it was very late and I didn't want to disturb you". This highlights that you have a life that your client is interrupting by calling out of hours, but you respect that **they** have a life and know good manners in not interrupting them!

Further Reading

- Hullomail – Smart voicemail in the cloud – http://tubb.co/1RDzedX

Using a call answering service

As a general rule, most people don't enjoy leaving messages on voicemail and are even worse at leaving good messages. How many times have you had a voicemail from a client that says: "Hi, can you call me please? Bye!"

What's the call about? Is it urgent? Can it wait until tomorrow? You'll never know until you call them back – and by then they've got their wish and they have you on the line to talk to.

By replacing voicemail with a human being at a call answering service, you'll be able to set clients' expectations better and improve communication.

For a small cost, call answering services allow you to redirect your calls – during evenings and weekends when you want to relax, during holidays and sick periods, and even during the day when you want some time for a meeting or planning – and send them to a human being at the call answering service who can set the callers' expectations over your availability and response time, and take a good quality message.

Instead of the standard message of "I'm not available, leave a message after the bleep" that clients get with voicemail, a call answering service can advise the caller that you're not available because you're in a meeting, having dinner with friends or family, out of the country, off sick or whatever other reason you give them to share with the caller. They can then set expectations on your response time and do what the client should have done in the first place – follow the guidelines you've provided them with for when and where to call depending on the hour of day or time of the week.

Call answering services are an additional expense for you and your business, but they give you a valuable buffer against clients who try to reach you at all hours – helping set those clients' expectations of your availability and response time and minimising any perceived confusion over your availability.

Further Reading

- Why your IT business should use a call answering service – http://tubb.co/1Gq5VQq
- Is your MSP service delivery crippled by being interrupt driven? – http://tubb.co/1MeTn6v

A word on "special" clients

For those clients who repeatedly insist on calling you out of hours or over weekends, even after you've been upfront and honest with them about your working hours, then the old phrase "Lack of planning on your part does not constitute an emergency on mine" springs to mind.

Just because your client has decided to work on an evening or weekend doesn't mean they dictate that you should too. You've already notified them of your working hours (by email and by written letter) so at the very least they should give you fair warning of their intentions and ask if they can contact you in the event of any issue out-of-hours.

You may be shaking your head at this point and saying "My client would **never** allow me to ignore them in that way!" I can assure you that the only reason that is the case is because you **allow** your clients to call you in this way. Nobody realistically expects you to be available 24x7x365 – but if you allow clients to call you at all hours, they will!

Draw the line, set expectations clearly – and when you're finished with work, put it out of your mind and re-charge.

And if you have a client who doesn't respect those boundaries and thinks they are somehow "special" then give serious consideration to your relationship with that client and ask yourself what life for your business would look like without them.

Plan your weekends

What does your typical weekend look like? If it's collapsing in an exhausted wreck from the week, slumped in front of the television virtually unable to move then you'll probably find that you often arrive at Monday morning thinking, "Where did the weekend go?" and feeling at best uninspired and at worse thoroughly gloomy about tackling a new week at work.

If you'd like your weekends to re-energise you – both physically and mentally – then plan them in advance.

I don't mean make plans to catch up on your laundry, shopping or housework – I mean make plans to have fun, do things that interest you and spend time with people you enjoy the company of.

For the most part, "doing nothing" doesn't make us happy and can leave us feeling lethargic and uninspired. But if we make plans – to spend time with friends or family, enjoy a meal out, go to the cinema, spend time doing hobbies, go away for the weekend and many other activities of this nature – we enjoy ourselves a lot more.

Planning and taking the time to do just a handful of things we enjoy can mean the difference between feeling like the weekend was enjoyable and well spent, or a weekend that just sort of happened.

Don't leave it until Friday to make plans; make them during the week. Speaking to friends and family to make arrangements adds to the anticipation and gives you something to look forward to – and motivation to resist the urge to work over the weekend.

Planning to have a good weekend is not only fun, good for you personally and good for your relationships with friends and family, but it will have a beneficial effect on your business as you return to work on a Monday full of energy and ideas and ready to make the week a success!

Chapter 12: Making it all work

What you've just read (unless you skipped straight to this chapter to see how this all ends!) is a collection of thoughts, tips, guidance and strategies that I've collected over ten years of being an IT business owner myself, and another five years of directly working with IT business owners to help them get ahead in business and life.

If there is one thing I want you to take away from this book, it's this. Being the owner of an IT business is tough, so be kind to yourself by being realistic about what you can and cannot do, and by being intentional about how you work and live.

If you put any one of the ideas in this book into practice, you'll notice an immediate improvement in the amount of time and energy you have as a business owner. I'd recommend you then try using that new found buffer to put into practice another one of the ideas I've shared in this book, and then another, until eventually this becomes a book that you've not just read, but are living.

You'll definitely notice the changes. Instead of merely surviving the trials and tribulations of running an IT business, you'll start to thrive. If you feel that you currently no longer enjoy being your own boss, you may find that having a more structured approach to your day-to-day activities allows you to find the joy in your work again.

You won't be the only one who notices a difference. Those around you will notice the positive changes and start to be influenced by them too. The wife of one of my IT business owner clients approached me recently to thank me. "Since you've worked with him, he's been less stressed, been home to spend time with his family," she told me. "We even took a holiday where he actually relaxed!"

Being the owner of an IT business is tough. But it doesn't have to be. By being realistic about the challenges you face, you can be intentional about how you tackle those challenges every day.

I hope this book acts not only as a survival guide for you as an IT business owner, enabling you to thrive, but also arms you with the tactics that will enable you to positively influence those around you – employees, clients, business partners, friends and family.

I'd love to hear your feedback and thoughts on this book, or for you to share your own journey with me. You can contact me on Twitter @tubblog, or drop me an email at richard@tubblog.co.uk

Are there any other topics you'd like to see me write about? Do us both a favour and visit my blog at www.tubblog.co.uk where I regularly share articles aimed at helping put IT business owners back in control. It may be there is already an article there that can help you, but if not, drop me a line with your question or thought and I may write a new article on the subject.

Finally, if you enjoyed this book and found it useful then I hope you'll consider leaving a review for it on your local Amazon site. Such reviews will help other IT business owners to find this book, and will help them to survive and thrive too.

I wish you the best of luck in growing your IT business and becoming a better leader!

About the Author

Richard Tubb is probably the most well-known face within the British IT Managed Service Provider (MSP) community. His track record speaks for itself, as he launched and sold his own MSP business before creating a leading MSP blog and consultancy practice.

As the former owner of an IT Managed Service Provider (MSP) business, Richard understands the challenges IT business owners face every day and can help you to overcome them while retaining what's left of your precious sanity.

Writer of the award-winning blog www.tubblog.co.uk, aimed at putting IT consultants back in control, you can find Richard on Twitter @tubblog.

Gratitude

I wish to personally thank the following people for their contributions to my inspiration and knowledge and to others for helping create this book.

Alan Matthews is my coach, mentor and friend and played a huge part in encouraging me to write this book and an even bigger part in kindly reading and editing the book for me.

Grace Marshall, Jo Harrison, Ryan Ashcroft and Alison Thompson all separately helped me with the practical steps of writing and publishing this book. I'm very grateful.

Neil Stark, Cathy Alper, Paul Tubb, Karen Strunks, Judith Burt and Gareth Brown all generously gave time out of their incredibly busy lives to read chapters and offer feedback.

Without Judith Burt, John Brown at Rogue Productions, and Holly Honeyford and the team at Madson Interim Solutions, I wouldn't have found the time to write this book at all. Thank you all for supporting me on a day-to-day basis.

Karl Palachuk and Manuel Palachuk -- you are two of my tech heroes who I'm now fortunate enough to consider friends. Thank you for encouraging me.

To John Shufflebottom, Gareth Brown and far too many other super-smart, super-successful and super-generous people I've known over the years – I appreciate how freely you've given of your time and experience throughout my journey in business and in life.

And to Claire, Mom, bruv and sis for believing in me when I often didn't myself and for picking me up when I'd fallen down. I love you.

Dedicated to the memory of my Dad, George Tubb. You taught me what legacy can mean.

Printed in Great
Britain
by Amazon